The original cover of the book

KEIDAN our Town in Lithuania

From the 50th Anniversary Souvenir Programme of the SOUTH AFRICAN
KEIDANER SICK BENEFIT AND BENEVOLENT SOCIETY (1900-1950)

First Published in 1950
by the Keidaner Sick, Benefit and Benevolent Society
to celebrate their 50th Anniversary.

Reprinted 2017

National Library of Australia Cataloguing-in-Publication entry

Title: Keidaner Sick, Benefit and Benevolent Society
        Originally compiled by the Keidan Sick Benefit and Benevolent Society in Johannesburg in 1950.(NB In English and Yiddish) ;
        Booklet now translated into English and reprinted in English;
        New booklet compiled by David Solly Sandler;
        Articles translated into English by Bella Golubchik, Aryeh Shcherbakov and Andrew Cassel

ISBN: 9780994619259 (paperback)

Subjects: Keidan Sick Benefit and Benevolent Society.
        Jews--Lithuania-- Keidan -History.
        Holocaust, Jewish (1939-1945)--Lithuania-- Keidan.
        Jews--South Africa--History
        South Africa--Emigration and immigration.

Other Creators/Contributors:
        Sandler, David Solly, compiler
        Golubchik, Bella, translator.
        Keidan Sick, Benefit and Benevolent Society, author.

Photo on Cover: The Keidan Market Place

Contact for book
David Solly Sandler <sedsand@iinet.net.au>

KEIDAN OUR TOWN IN LITHUANIA

FOREWORD

This book, *Keidan, Our Town In Lithuania,* commences with the Jewish history and life in Keidan and then focuses on the destruction of Jewish life in 1941 with the arrival of the Germans. It then focuses on the South African Keidaner Sick Benefit and Benevolent Society.

The book, is an adaptation of the *50th Anniversary Souvenir Programme of the South African Keidaner Sick Benefit and Benevolent Society.* While it includes all the contents of the *Souvenir Programme,* the order has been rearranged.

With the permission of Aryeh Shcherbakov and Andrew Cassel of the Israeli and Keidan Societies several articles, translations and photos from the *Keidan Yizkor Book* have been included for completeness.

A large proportion of *the Souvenir Programme,* was written in Yiddish and has now been translated into English thanks to Bella Golubchik, Aryeh Shcherbakov and Andrew Cassel.

CONTENTS

	Page	Original Pages
JEWISH LIFE IN KEIDAN AND ITS DESCRUCTION		
Five Hundred Years of Jewish Keidan	3	68-71 *(2)*
Memories (of Keidan) *by Sholom Dat (Johannesburg)*	10	*(1)*
Fire in the Town *by Itzhak Wolpe,*	12	57-59
My Town, Keidan *Nathan Berger (Meyer Yanusevers)*	16	60-61
The Destruction of Keidan *by David Wolpe*	19	47-50
Communal Buildings Destroyed by the Nazis	25	51
Among the Ruins *by Chaim Ronder*	29	*(1)*
THE KEIDAN HELPING HAND AND BENEVOLENT SOCIETY IN JOHANNESBURG		
Golden Jubilee of the Keidan Helping Hand and Benevolent Society in Johannesburg	32	41-45
The Keidaner Association In South Africa by *Max Rochin*	38	*(1)*
Deceased Landsleit and Members of Keidaner Society in Memoriam	40	53 *(2)*
The Late Mr Samuel Stein Pioneer and Philanthropist	42	21
The Stein Family in the US	43	31
Zvi Lipschitz, Hy"D *Ben-Moshe (Johannesburg)*	44	55
Greetings to the Keidaner Landsmanschaft Johannnesburg	45	15,16, 73,74 *(2)*
More Greetings	48	13 and 17
Prominent Keidaner Society Members Send Greetings	50	19
Greetings and Photos	51	23,25,27,33,35,37
The Keidaner Landsleit in Israel Beit Zera	57	72 *(2)*
Reunion of a well-known Keidanian family	58	29

Notes
(1) Articles from the Keidan Yizkor Book have been included for completeness with the permission of Aryeh Shcherbakov and Andrew Cassel of the Israeli and Keidan Societies.
(2) Article was previously in Yiddish in the Souvenir Programme - translated into English by Bella Golubchik

FIVE HUNDRED YEARS OF JEWISH KEIDAN
THE HISTORY OF THE KEIDANER JEWISH COMMUNITY

Keidan occupied the place of honour among the towns and shtetlach of the former Jewish Lithuania. It was one of the oldest and most renowned Jewish communities in Lithuania.

The fact that Keidan was associated with the names of two great historical personalities: The Vilner Gaon and Moshe Leib Lilienblum, would place Keidan in an exceptionally prominent position in the annals of the Jewish history of Lithuania, and also in the general history of Eastern European Jewry.

Jews were already living in Keidan in the fifteenth century. The history of the Jews of Keidan goes back nigh on 500 years.

As soon as the Jews arrived, when they had not yet settled in their new home, there was a decree by the Grand Duke Aleksander, that all Jews should leave Lithuania. The new Jewish community in Keidan was ruined. Most of them resettled in Poland on the Lithuanian border.

In 1503, the Jews were permitted to return to Lithuania, but only a small number of the expelled Jews of Keidan returned there.

In the 16th century, Keidan was the domicile of the Grand Dukes Radzivill. The Radzivills were Calvinists, and fought against Catholicism. Christopher Radzivill wanted to enlarge the Jewish population in Keidan in order to increase trade. He therefore permitted the Jews all civil rights and also guaranteed that no one would lose ownership of property if he translocated to another town.

However, Radzivill wanted to allow only people with good character references and assurances of honesty. Consequently the Jews who came, were predominantly from Germany and were specially selected educated people and from the privileged class.

There is an assumption, that many of the Jews who came to Keidan at that time, were those who had been banished from Scotland among whom were a great number of weavers. That is why such a wonderful weaving industry developed in Keidan. At the beginning of the 19th century, the weaving industry was exclusively in the hands of the Jews.

The Grand Duke Radzivill welcomed the new immigrants very warmly and set aside a special part of the town for them.

Moshe Leib Lilienblum : Leader of the "Chovevei Tzion Movement", was born and lived in Keidan.

> Keidaner Jews have always regarded themselves as superior.
>
> If one were asked : "Where do you come from?" He would answer with pride : "Who? Me? I am a Keidaner". And when uttering the word "I" he would jab his chest with his thumb. The other Lithuanian Jews, envious of them, named them "Ich Keidaner – with an indentation in the heart" The "indentation, that is, which came from poking their chests with their finger.
>
> The Keidaner were also renowned for their great erudition and sat hunched over the Gemorrah constantly studying. So they were also named "The hunchbacks".
>
> Other jokers said that the Keidaner backs became hunched from poking their chests with their fingers. That is, when they banged on their chests, their backs hunched over.

A view of the entrance to the Shtetl, from "The other side of the water"

The immigrants developed different styles of handicrafts and Radzivill was very proud of them.

Many very religiously educated Jews came in from Germany and the Jewish community in Keidan became a centre of Torah and religious observance.

The Jews in Lithuania and Zamut decided to establish a separate "Committee of the Main Lithuanian States", which had representation on the "Committee of the Four States" and Keidaner Jews were represented on the "Va'ad d"Lita" just a few years after its establishment.

The Grand Duke Janosh Radzivill was also friendly towards the Jews and continued to allow them all the same privileges and civil rights that his father, Christopher, had given them.

The Jews were then a most esteemed and important element in civil and economic life in Keidan. They were engaged in the wine trade and in brewing, money lending, export and import, agriculture and various trades

The Jewish artisans were organised into various guilds, which bore the same duties as the non-Jewish guilds. Jews were represented on the Town Council, where they used to determine levies and taxes. They also oversaw the fair subdivision of tax monies among the Jews, as among the Christians.

Every year, the Jews had to undergo military training exercises under the supervision of an official from the Magistrate.

The streets where the Jews lived were: The Old Market Street, Smilger Street, The Jewish Lane and The Crooked Lane.

In April 1652, Radzivill issued a decree, that all Jewish butchers and ritual butchers of Kosher meat, and all those who handled beef cattle for butchering, should organise themselves into a guild.

The bloody historical events of the years 1608 and 1609 ("T'ach V't'at") did not touch Keidan. The Keidaner Community sent support for the affected suffering Jews.

In the middle of the 17th century, the Jewish community suffered a great deal from the victorious Polish armies, which conquered Karl Gustav, who was supported by Yanosh Radzivill. The Poles regarded the Jews as traitors and supporters of the Calvinist Radzivills.

Bagoslav Radzivill, the successor to Yanosh, confirmed all the civil rights of the Jews in Keidan. On 11th June 1662, the "Starosta Avorski" reported to Arch Duke Radzivill that notwithstanding the command of Arch Duke Bagoslavus not to annul Jewish rights, the Catholic Bishop wished to announce that it was now forbidden for Keidaner Jews to work for Christians.

This stemmed from the accusation of a certain Stefan Balshetis against the Keidaner Jews, to the Commisar of Radzivill's Palace, in 1686, stating that they did not observe the law to close their businesses on Sundays and that they had spread themselves over the whole town ignoring the limits on the quarters that had been set aside for their occupation. He also said that the Jews had become more powerful and richer in Keidan and that they had overstepped the limits which were incumbent on them.

The Railway Station in Keidan

Because of the great tribulations and persecutions of the Jews in the various countries of Europe, Reb Yossel Kobrinerin, a great scholar in Keidan, promulgated a "S'lichah" – a prayer begging G-d for forgiveness in 1698, which was added to the liturgy in all congregations of Lithuania and Zamut.

The Russo–Swedish War in 1704, also had severe repercussions on the Jewish community in Keidan, which had become so impoverished that they were forced to borrow money from the landowners, to cover the congregational expenses. It is told, that a certain landowner, named Gurski, to whom the community in Keidan was indebted for a few thousand zlotys, locked the Shul on Shabbat while the Jews were 'davening' and imprisoned them there. They managed to defer until after Shabbat when they managed to arrange the payments.

In 1721, Keidan was the 3rd most important among the significant communities in Lithuania/Zamut. At that time the whole personal tax in Lithuania was worth 60 thousand zlotys.

The following were the contributions: Brisk: 5150 zlotys, Grodno: 4500, Keidan: 4300, Pinsk: 3730, Minsk: 1300, Vilna: 1100.

In 1727, The "Brisker Rov" Rav Avrohom Katzenellenbogen, a son of the "Keidaner Rov" Rav Dovid Katzenellenbogen, came to Vilna. Vilna at that time could not stop singing the praises of the "Wunderkind", Eliyahu, the son of the Vilner scholar, Rabbi Sh'lomo Zalman. When Reb Avrohom heard the six year old genius, he could not but be amazed at him, and begged his father, Reb Dovid, to allow the child to accompany him (Reb Avrohom) to Keidan, where his father, Reb Dovid, should study with him. The subsequent Vilner Gaon, Reb Eliyahu, studied and was nurtured in Keidan throughout his whole youth. He married the daughter of a wealthy Keidaner, Reb Yehuda.

At the end of the 18th century The Jewish way of life in Keidan was the same as that of all the Jewish communities in Lithuania. The main "role-players" (communal leaders) led the community together with the elected heads. "Torah was the best merchandise". The Beit Din in Keidan was always one of the greatest of the generation. The Yeshiva and the chedorim were always full. They studied day and night in the Batei Medrash. The whole environment was filled with Torah and religious observance.

In 1784 the Keidaner congregation built the Big shul together with the new Beit Medrash. They employed the best craftsmen to create a carved Aron Kodesh (Holy Ark for the Torah Scrolls) and to decorate the vault and the ceiling of the shul. The Aron Kodesh

This illustrates when the Nevyaisz'ah overflowed its banks. This flooding, which happened annually at Pesach time, inundated almost half the Shtetl. This photo shows the Market place under water.

Horwitz's pharmacy and Reb Motte the Ironmonger's business in the centre of Keidan.

which occupied a whole third part of the "Eastern Wall" was composed of artistic engravings of flowers, animals and birds, painted and gilded. It also contained an "Eternal Hebrew calendar".

In one of the carved columns of the Aron Kodesh, under a glass cover, inscribed on parchment, was the name of the Prime Motivator, the person who did the most, who was instrumental in the building of the shul and the Beit Medrash, Reb Avrohom Evli, and the year of completion of the work, 1807.

There was a very large sun dial, with Hebrew letters, on the stone gateway of the shul yard.

In 1795, after the Third Partition of Poland, Keidan and the whole of Lithuania, were transferred to Russia. In 1804, Aleksander the First, decreed the expulsion of the Jews from the villages. A large number of impoverished settlers , who had been chased out of the shtetlach, arrived in Keidan.

This increased the number of saloon keepers, but mainly, it created a large number of gardeners and orchard keepers. The Keidaner green vegetables, particularly cucumbers, were renowned throughout the whole of Zamut.

The Napoleonic/Russian War in 1812, caused a great deal of damage in Keidan. Most of the Lithuanian Jews, as also the Keidaner, sided with Russia, and rejoiced in the downfall of Napoleon's armies. Particularly because the Catholic Poles and their clergy strongly supported the French, they were infuriated with the Jews.

The great struggle, which was taking place in other parts of Lithuania, between the Chassidim and the Mltnagdim, did not affect Keidan. The community was very religiously observant and led by leaders who closely guarded against any religious innovations being instituted.

The notebooks of the artisans paint an interesting picture of the life and times of the Keidaner community.

On the first day of Rosh Hashannah, a tailor appeared in the shul, wearing a silk skull cap (yarmulkah). This enraged the elite community leaders, the privileged who sat at the "Eastern Wall", and who contended that only they were entitled to wear such yarmulkahs. So enraged were they, that they sent the beadle to the offending tailor immediately after the service to bring him to the committee room and fined him. He had to contribute ten pounds of candles to the shul and relinquish the yarmulkah.

This punishment was hugely insulting to all the artisans of Keidan, who were united in their guilds from ancient times. So, on the first day of Sukkot, there entered the shul, not only tailors, but also shoemakers, furriers, hatters and other tradespeople, all wearing new silk yarmulkahs, fur edged Chassidic hats, satin robes, tied with long belts, dressed up in fancy garb, exactly like the upper class citizens who sat at the Eastern Wall, and probably attired even more gloriously. This is how they appeared on Sukkot, to the disgust of the elite gentlemen, who sat at the Eastern Wall.

This however, cost the Keidaner artisans dearly.

On the first day, of the intermediate days of Sukkot, Graf Tshafskis Haidukas, took all the artisans into the central warehouse yard and caned them all. This particular type of humiliation united all the tradesmen in a "Holy War" against the communal leaders. This struggle was even transferred into the judicial administration of the Russian government. However, the committee had the means to "grease" their palms and the power of such graft nullified all the efforts of the artisans. This struggle endured for years and cost both sides thousands of Roubles.

Subsequently, the tradesmen saw that they couldn't achieve anything against the communal leaders so they undertook a new path of action. When they encountered representatives of the leaders in the forest, or the countryside, they taught them a good lesson by giving them a smart beating. The communal leaders then decided to make peace with the artisans. They sent a Shamash to negotiate. The tradespeople set the following conditions :

Firstly : That the silk yarmulkah ,and the satin gown and long belt, could be freely worn by any Jew.

Secondly, if there was an arbitration in the Beit Din between an artisan and a rich homeowner, there should be a judge (Dayan) stating the case for the worker, also that the tradespeople should have representation in the communal chamber.

The communal leaders consented to these negotiations and thus, peace was concluded between the "Eastern Wall" and the "Western Wall".

As a result of this struggle, a small shul, called "Chayei Adam" was established for the workers, where they had their own "Eastern Wall", and their own Dayan. He used to study a page of Talmud with them between the Afternoon and Evening prayer Services. Also on Friday at twilight, after the meal and on Shabbat after the service, he would expound on the Biblical Portion of the Week.

A few score years later, the richest tailor in Keidan, Eliyahu Vilner, permitted them to build a little shul, where the artisans and the butchers could pray together.

The Polish revolution of 1831 did not miss Keidan out. There was a very heavy exchange of fire between the retreating Poles and the pursuing Russian armies.

One summer Shabbat evening, when the Shul was full of worshippers, a cannon ball was shot by the Russians, into the Eastern Wall of the Shul, through the ceiling and over the Aron Kodesh The missile flew over the heads of the Jews and exited the Shul, not having injured even one of those praying.

This was considered to be a miracle and the hole in the Eastern Wall was left unrepaired as a sign of the miracle for future generations.

The Jews of Keidan experienced the same tribulations, as did all the other communities under the tyrannical rule of Nicholas the First. The kidnapping of Jewish children to fill the annual quota of army numbers for which Keidan was liable, began at this time.

The Haskallah Movement (The Enlightenment Movement) infiltrated Keidan, that stronghold of Torah and Jewish Observance, and enticed whoever they could of the youth, to the distress of their parents.

In 1843, Reb Hirsheh Bender, a poor man but a very learned scholar, fathered a son, Moshe Leib. This only son, who his father began teaching at a very early age, grew up to be a genius. The father was studying a religious book with the congregation, in Eliyahu Vilner's little shul and the very young child, Moshe Leib already founded a group to study the same "Ein Ya'akov". This child grew up to be the famously enlightened leader of the "Chovevei Tzion" movement and the eminent Hebrew writer, Moshe Leib Lilienblum.

In 1846, Pesach Smilg fathered a son, who later became one of the most eminent of Jewish scholars, Dr Yosef Smilg.

In 1857, the Keidaner congregation engraved the name of Graf Marian Tshafski, on a marble tablet in the shul, as a token of their appreciation for his friendship towards the Jews, as he had donated the bricks for the building of the new Beit Medrash. They also presented him with a silver goblet, and the official, Shlomo Berenshtain, presented him with an illuminated address in Hebrew, German and French.

In the eighties, when the pogroms against the Jews spread over Russia a great exodus of Russian Jews began. Many Keidaner emigrated to America, England and South Africa, where great numbers of landsleit gathered together.

Political Zionism, which came into existence at the end of the 19th century, also the Socialist Bund, found enthusiastic supporters in Keidan. The persecutions and pogroms against the Jews by the Tzarists caused more Jews to emigrate and the Jewish community in Keidan was greatly reduced before the First World War. The dire economic situation was also a contributing factor.

During the first winter of the war, in 1914, many Jews from the surrounding shtetlach, fled to Keidan. In March of 1915, the Russian Regime began expelling Jews from Lithuania, chasing them deep into Russia.

In Keidan, the command was given, on May 16th, that every Jew without exception was to leave the town, and be gone by midnight on 18th May. Any Jew found there after this time would be hanged.

The Jewish community in Keidan was immediately uprooted. Most of them arrived in Vilna, others fled into deepest Russia and Zogor in Siberia.

The Christian population soon apportioned all the Jewish belongings and possessions among themselves.

When the Germans entered Vilna, the Keidaner Jews who were there, received permission to return to Keidan, and they began once more to rebuild the ravaged Jewish property.

After the War, many exiled Keidan Jews returned from Russia and began to rebuild their lives.

With the rebuilding of an independent Lithuania, Keidan became a main hub and began to develop very fast. The Jewish community rebuilt with renewed vigour. Industries were revived. Outstanding leather workshops, also Mills and brickworks, Hebrew and Yiddish Folkshuls and kindergartens were all established and also a Hebrew Pro-Gymnasia, a large library with Hebrew and Yiddish books, Parties and Cultural Organisations – on the right and on the left of politics and a Yiddish Folksbank which supported Jewish artisans and shopkeepers.

Keidan played an outstanding role in the period of Jewish autonomy, as one of the most important communities in Lithuania.

In 1939, after the outbreak of the war between Germany and Poland, the Jewish refugees found a warm welcome in Keidan. A yeshiva consisting of 150 Yeshiva students, from the famous Mir Yeshiva, was established; also a kibbutz of refugees from the youth movement HaShomer HaTza'ir. The Keidan community helped them settle in. At the outbreak of War Keidan numbered 3000 souls, in a general population of ten thousand.

The outbreak of the Soviet/Nazi war, led to the terrible tragedy of total destruction and annihilation of the Jewish community in Keidan which took place in the middle of the 20th century.

The material in this overview has been taken from the anthology "KEIDAN" published by the Keidaner Society in New York edited by B Ch Kassel and Dr Ch Y Epshtain.

Translated into English by Bella Golubchik

The wooden bridge over the Nevyaisz'a

MEMORIES (of Keidan) *by Sholom Dat (Johannesburg)*

Keidan is one of the oldest cities in Lithuania, and her Jewish community was also one of the first.

Keidan was originally a small fishing settlement, which was started in the mid-14th century by the Neviazhe river, where the Abele, Datnovke and Smilga streams flow into it.

The settlement at first had the name of its founder, Kazdan. Later it began to be called by its Lithuanian name, "Keidainiai".

In the 15th century Keidan grew in importance. In the last quarter of the century the Jewish community began to organise. But it was short-lived, because the Keidan Jews along with all the Jews of Lithuania in 1495 were forced into exile by order of the chieftain Alexander. When the Jews were permitted to return in 1503, not many Jews evidently settled in Keidan.

Christopher Radzivil, Lithuanian prince and "voivode" of Vilna, in 1614 received half of Keidan as a dowry from his father in law, Stanislav Kishko (in 1490 the Lithuanian-Russian family Kishko received all of Keidan as a gift from the Polish king, Casimir IV). Later, he purchased the other half. Wishing to increase commerce in Keidan, he issued an order, according to which Jews were granted civil and religious rights. This, naturally, attracted a great number of Jews. The new immigrants came mostly from Germany.

Janusz Radzivil later confirmed all the privileges the Jews had had from his father Christopher. In his time, around the middle of the 17th century, Jews occupied the most important positions in the town's economic life. They were involved in wine-making and brewing, money lending, farming and various crafts.

With small interruptions, because of various wars which the town endured and because of epidemics, such as cholera, the Jewish population in Keidan began to develop more and more. In the 1880's, Jews from Keidan first began to emigrate, mainly to the United States.

Keidan prided itself on its lineage – and a lineage it had. For example, Keidan had the oldest pharmacy in all of the Baltics. It had been in existence more than 275 years, while the oldest pharmacy in Moscow is only 200 years old.

Keidan possessed an old, brick synagogue – done in an old style, with a beautifully carved ark, with clocks and tablets, with beautiful, although barely visible paintings. Alongside the synagogue, still standing, is the "lock-up" where the community used to confine criminals.

Keidan consistently had great rabbis and outstanding scholars. The Vilna Gaon studied there in his youth, with the noted rabbi David, son of Reb Ezekiel Katzenellenbogen, the author of "Knesses Ezekiel."

The well-known writer M L Lilienblum was also a native of Keidan. The town was always full of sages and scribes. (A fine work about Keidan was published by Boruch Chaim Cassel in the book "Keidan," New York, 1930.)

***

It is now many years since I left my town of Keidan. I am now decades away from my native town, living in big, modern Johannesburg – and yet a deep longing won't stop piercing my heart for the little rooftops of Keidan, for the moss that stopped up the winter windows, for the study-house, for all the good and pious Jews of the town.

Here, in the centrally heated apartments I am reminded often of the simple brown and white tiled ovens in which people steamed their *cholents.* Family and neighbours would sit around in the long winter evenings, and especially on the pleasant Friday nights, or at twilight on Shabbat, talking about current affairs and describing the wonders of America and Europe.

It can't be forgotten, how in the freezing winter cold, Jewish mothers would chop out a hole in the Smilga to soak their laundry. I can still hear exactly, as if it were today, the sound of the rolling pins in the matzo bakery.

And who doesn't remember the military conscription days in the town, when Christian draftees would celebrate all over town with music and singing, and trembling Jewish boys would sit with their hearts pounding, that God forbid they should be taken "into the soldiers"?

In Keidan it was custom, when a Jewish boy was before the draft board, he would signal through the window to his waiting mother whether or not he was "taken." Drawing the hand across the throat meant: slaughtered! More than one mother broke out crying, "my tree, my hero, my breadwinner."

It is interesting, by the way, to recall that the famous enemy of the Jews and Russian prime minister Stolypin was for a time the chairman of the draft board in Keidan (he had a farm not far from the town). And, not to compare, but Morris Winchevsky also had a connection with the Keidan draft board: in 1877 he stood before it and was rejected, having sufficiently "starved" himself beforehand.

In 1914 a great fire broke out in Keidan, which destroyed the town from the bridge to Long Street, from the market to the synagogue-yard. This was a kind of prelude to the First World War, which also brought disaster to the Jews of Keidan, who on May 16 [1915] received an order giving them two days to leave the town. The expulsion sent a long procession of Jews to Vilna, while others ended up deep inside Russia.

Returning from the expulsion, the Jews started rebuilding their destroyed and ruined town, demonstrating a trust in the good will of a newly independent Lithuania -- a trust which in time was totally betrayed.

First published in "Lita" Copyright 1951, by the Jewish-Lithuanian Cultural Society Inc..

Translation by A. Cassel Keidan yizkor book, page 169

Copyright © Keidan Memorial Fund 2016

The palace of the renowned Graf Totleben, looks out over the Park.
Below the Park "The Datnovah" is visible.

FIRE IN THE TOWN by Yitzhak Wolpe, as told to David Wolpe

1.

It was 1914, late spring, just a week after the holiday of Shavuot. The air in our small town was light, sunny and fragrant. To us children the days were like giant, blue-speckled flowers with burning golden centers. And the nights, filled with sweet, intoxicating breezes, would rock us to sleep amid silver dreams.

It was on one such night—whether it was after Shabbat, or else just an ordinary Wednesday, I can't now recall—that the comfortable fabric of my dreams was ripped asunder by a familiar but frightened voice:

"Wake the children, quick! Yitzhak ... Itsikl, get up! My child, the house is on fire!"

Mother stood by my bed, looking pale, her blue eyes tearful.

I bolted up and sat, confused, on the edge of my bed, not knowing what was happening. Through the windowpane a dreadful light flapped crimson wings, clawing at our windows with a menacing blackness.

"What is it, Mama?" I stammered, barely able to cry out.

"Take the little children and run with them to Grandma's! Father and I may still be able to save something."

I was not yet twelve years old, but suddenly I found myself thrown into adulthood. There was danger. I had to help. I had responsibility ... a job to do ... duty! In that instant I became a grown-up. Fear left me. I quickly put on my short pants and jacket, and stood ready, no longer terrified by the flames climbing in at the windows. Now I know that on that night my fate was sealed, and the course of my later life set. From that night I became an independent person. And in our home, life was never the same again.

My smallest brother, Elimelekh, still an infant, was still lying in bed. The next oldest, Avraham, was also still a small, helpless child. Mother packed up both children and entrusted them to my care. I left the house with them. It was a mild summer midnight. As long as I live I won't forget that night.

The neighboring house was engulfed in flames and smoke; it crackled like a dry pile of kindling. Jews cursed and ran around like poisoned mice, back and forth; women moaned and writhed – it appeared the town had gone completely mad.

Through the tumult and confusion I strained with all my senses not to lose my little brothers. The horrible scene was reflected in their eyes, and in my childish heart there was only sadness. The house of our neighbor the tar dealer was burning like a torch, and the air turned sharp and biting from the tar smoke. I ran with the little ones to the middle of the market square, where we fell, exhausted, to the ground.

The fire had spread among the other houses. Women ran around holding small children in their arms, and men carried bundles of bedding. There was much wailing as everything was already enveloped in flame. My little heart grew heavier as I waited nervously for Father and Mother to arrive. The flickering light of the fire was reflected in my brothers' innocent faces, like the wings of a trapped bird...

I gathered up my courage and waited. Waited and watched over the little ones, like a faithful dog watches over his master's property. In my childish head was only one thought, repeated endlessly: Nothing must happen to the children!

So we stayed and waited for a long time in the middle of the market square, while the fire devoured one house after another. With me then was one more stunned and confused person, my older sister Esther. But mother had entrusted the children to me, and I felt it was I who carried the responsibility for them. And indeed, the children remained safe.

Only in the morning, when daylight flooded the smoking ruins of the town, was I able to read in Father's sad face and Mother's weeping eyes what an enormous tragedy had occurred. I ran out into the street, but was forced to come back immediately because the scene in the street oppressed me fearfully: Our house, the workshop, the store and warehouse had been wiped out, without a trace. But the fire had been put out here, right by our shop; everything beyond it remained intact. Father and Mother had saved only a little merchandise from the store before the fire reached it.

From then our troubles began, one after the other, linked in a chain, like a punishment from on high upon our family.

2.

Right after the fire we moved in with my grandma Leah, my mother's mother. Such a pious woman was hard to find even in those days. She was a saint who asked for nothing in this life, a woman whose heart held nothing but goodwill and mercy for all, strangers as well as her own kin. She gave charity anonymously, and devoted herself to raising her children, instilling in them a spirit of goodness and honesty. I still recall how proud it made me, even as a little boy, to hear people speak of my grandma's virtues. More than once I heard it said that such a fine woman, a woman without a mean bone in her body, came along once in ten generations, and I was fortunate to be in her presence daily.

But then Father became terribly sick. Our misfortune had dealt him too hard a blow; the colossal exertion and stress during the fire had ruined his health, and in a short time left him wrecked in body and spirit. He needed to be taken to a major specialist in a large city, or so decreed the doctors of our little town. There he had to remain several weeks in a clinic, under the constant care of the medical professionals there. And quite miraculously, Father returned to health and became himself again.

But a new affliction already awaited our family. On the very day that father left the hospital, as we awaited him with happy hearts, war was declared, the Great War of 1914. And right away, before he even had a chance to get home, he was obliged to report to the military. That was the order: to immediately report for duty in whatever district one happened to be at the time.

We had hopes at first that Father, following such a serious illness, would not be taken from us. But we all were bitterly disappointed, as Father was quickly drafted and mobilized. He had been born in St. Petersburg and spoke a fine, polished Russian, and that proved his undoing. The army needed educated men like him immediately, the military commission declared, and they dispatched him straightaway to Grodno.

On Mother's shoulders descended the burden of making a living and at the same time caring for five small children. We children felt as though we had been robbed of the precious and beloved thing we called Daddy. Our longing for him doubled and multiplied with each passing day. We didn't exactly know what it was that had torn our father from us, but we heard the grown-ups talking of something called a war, and we came to understand that this thing, war, was to blame.

Consumed with the daily chores and troubles, Mother no longer had time to care for us, and we were left suddenly without the warmth and tenderness that other children enjoyed. As the oldest, I, a twelve-year-old, was suddenly launched into a new life, the tough life of a grown-up. I was appointed head of the household.

Like an apple grows ripe in the sun, so did I, in a short time, grow ripe from troubles. Childish games and pastimes ceased to interest me. Our life turned joyless as I earnestly took up the functions of household head, who had to worry about his little brothers. Carrying responsibilities that were greater than my years strengthened my spirit and energy, and in some ways tamed and replaced my childhood yearnings.

Mother had it very hard. But the stress and loneliness never made her bitter, and she never was heard complaining about her fate. No task was too difficult if it was for us, and she never appeared jealous or held a grudge against the neighbors whose lot was far better than ours.

With the little bit of merchandise that had been rescued and a little saved-up cash, Mother restarted the business. She would stand in the store until late in the evening, while I stayed in the workshop, keeping an eye on the children. In the quiet hours when they played or slept, I would help with the sewing. Our workshop and our living quarters were together. We had a cap factory, where we sewed hats and other fur goods. Learning that trade well as a young boy gave me a certain self-confidence in later life.

By then I understood what a war was, and that Father probably would not be coming home soon, and I accustomed myself to a stone-hard life, devoid of ordinary childish joys and hopes. Late at night, tired, I would fall asleep with sorrow gnawing at my heart; I knew that we lacked the love that other children had, but Mother's pale blue eyes, moist with gratitude, gave me quiet comfort.

"My child, my Itsikl," she would say, "you're my only support now. My beloved child, may the Lord reward you with happiness and success in your life."

That small bit of mother-love sustained me in those days.

3.

That life made me an old child, with a sense of judgement and responsibility. I came to understand that working more meant earning more, and earning more meant living better. One had to exert oneself, so we contracted to sew for the military, and I became a little entrepreneur. This didn't come easily to me, because all the businesslike calculations required years of experience. And very often I would find myself feeling helpless and inferior, not knowing how to handle our problems. That deeply affected my mood and spirit.

I also had to do the hard housework – carrying water from the nearby river, cutting wood and lighting the oven, putting the children to bed and rocking them to sleep at night. We more than filled up the little house, so I had to sleep with my brother Avraham above the stove ...

Nearly a year went by. The river behind our home dried up. Outside it turned warm, and mild breezes blew. With the coming of spring our souls grew lighter, and it seemed to me that new hope would sprout for our family.

Around Passover our family was destined to grow larger: We were getting a new little brother, and we children took the news with great rejoicing. This brought a new division of labor among us; my sister, still then a little girl, had to take over Mother's duties in the shop. It was pitiful to observe such a dainty creature dealing all day with the village peasants, who were typically drunk and coarse. My authority as head of the house broadened, with vastly increased responsibiilties: Watching over the children and acting as both nanny and tutor, besides helping with the sewing; carrying water and tending the fire, all as before. Still, that year, I would sometimes steal a few minutes late in the evening to read a storybook. I had had to give up my schooling early – there was no time or opportunity for it – but reading was for me like a glimpse into a beautiful, carefree world, each book a magic land to be discovered. Dead tired, I would fall asleep late by the weak night-lamp and creep above the oven to my "bed." Awakening in the morning, I would try to recall the stories and in my childish way, fantasize about their further course ...

Passover came and went. And again the blooming blue days and nights of silver graced our poor little town, like a magic charm hanging overhead. For reasons I couldn't then comprehend, our baby brother didn't have his circumcision on time, and it was already getting toward Shavuot again. Mother said: "Already a year since our great misfortune! Perhaps, my little joy, you will bring luck to our home?" And her tear-streaming eyes beamed at the baby's face, which was already red from crying.

The days were restless. Jews bustled about, whispering assorted rumors of pogroms and harsh government decrees that were occurring in other towns and villages, and were likely to make their way here as well soon.

The air became dense and black, laden with heavy clouds. Our little town filled up with soldiers, who took over market and the surrounding streets when the military barracks ran out of room. The Jewish houses became sad and cheerless as hordes of booted, bearded, cursing Russians spread fear among the people. Here and there the Cossacks assaulted Jews, taking their money and merchandise, and issuing "assurances" that the time was soon coming when they would make an end of the "*zhids*" ... Jews sat in their houses as if on hot coals, and waited for salvation.

No salvation came. Instead, there came an order from the military high command, that within three days, all Jews had to leave Kovno province.

"What are we to do now? How can we travel, for who knows how long, with a baby not yet circumcised?" Mother's grief burst out, and she ran around madly seeking advice from rabbis and others.

Despite all the confusion, when word got out that the circumcision was still to be performed, all the women of the town gathered at our house. As I recall it, each one asked that the baby be named for a near relative or friend, suggesting that the namesake had been of such merit that his heavenly worth would help us survive our ordeal.

"Such righteousness will help us all, Chaye-Libe my dearest! ... Name him after my grandpa, do you hear? He was a holy man, a saint!" Thus did the women argue their cases, each trying to convince my mother of the great merit of their sanctified uncles or aunts. But Mother was not impressed.

The honor was finally given to Sara-Leah, a cousin of granny Badanes (father's mother), who named the baby after her husband. The circumcision was performed two days before we left, in haste and fear amid the boxes and bedding. Our things were already packed for the journey, and there we were, having a celebration – but quietly, secretly, lest we arouse the curiosity of the gentiles and the thieving Cossacks. And so we quit our little town carrying a new little brother who had a new name – Yisrael.

We traveled different paths, however. Because of the baby's recent circumcision, Mother had to travel with all her children on the train that the government had prepared to evacuate the Jews. It was a terrible hardship, traveling right after a circumcision in a crowded rail carriage, with no water or medications to be found. Upon my back fell the responsibility for the few poor possessions we had left. There was no one else to rely on but me, the oldest in the family, so we hired a cart, on which we packed up all the household items and the merchandise. And down the highway, through towns already half-abandoned by Jews, I and the wagon driver ventured off, exiles in the world. We dragged ourselves through the heat and dust to Vilna.

I had just turned twelve years old, but I was already the family guardian.

It was three days before Shavuot. The fields made me drunk with their sweet spring smells. I lay half-slumbering, my insides rocking back and forth with the goods and my heart repressing tears. I felt lonely and lost, but I knew that I had to watch over the property that had been entrusted to me. I understood that this was all we had, and from this we had to earn our living until Father returned from the war.

On the road we had to stop, hide in the woods or drive out of our way in order to avoid the villages, where gentiles were known to have robbed Jews. Because of the fear of thieves our short trip took much longer, and Mother was beside herself with worry. Eventually, however, our long wanderings ended and we came safely to Vilna, and Mother greeted us with tears of joy.

Copyright © Keidan Memorial Fund 2017
Translated by A Cassel.
Keidan Yizkor Book pp 144-8

Managers, Board and staff of the Yiddishe Folk's Bank in Keidan in 1926.

MY TOWN, KEIDAN *Nathan Berger (Meyer Yanusevers)*

With simple words, in a few score lines
I will set down, to preserve the memory
of how a town endured for generations,
how Jews lived during the twenties.

About a town that was once in Lithuania,
with woods and fields, green without end.
A town with people, a lot of them Jews,
although it was certainly no big city.

With its three rivers, three mills, and a nobleman's orchard,
a train that used to stop twice a day
tooting its whistle to announce its arrival from far parts
to the town three kilometers away.

With cement sidewalks, the streets were paved.
A fire brigade mustered and
practiced, hoping for the chance
to put out a blaze in some peasant's barn.

Boys and girls would go walking together
on the town bridge or in the Borer woods.
Couples in love would express their affection
on grassy lawns in the town's fields.

***

Keidan was a Jewish town
that had acquired a reputation across the world.
Famous rabbis and scholars
were born, lived and died there.

A "Jacob's Well" society, a "Bachelors' Crown" group,
Rabbis gave lectures in the yeshiva.
There were "*Yavne*" and "*Tarbut*" and the government high schools
The Maccabee club, Hashomer Hatzair and even Bundists.

And in the old prayer house, at the center of the town
more happened than sermons and prayers to God
there Zundl Ginzburg, the *gabbai*, distributed *aliyas*
and the Tailors' Society elected cantors.

Jews would come there to hear the latest news
Meetings were held to vote yay or nay
(since arguments broke out often
some siding with the rabbi, others with the judge.)

***

And a lot happened all around town

There was a market each Thursday, a fair every year.
The town would rumble like Shlapobersky's mill,
People bought horses, and livestock, and pigs' bristles.

Moshe the hatter would be sewing away,
Nissan the potter would be turning his wheel,
and Moteh the blacksmith would hammer and hammer
making shoes for the horses and plows for the fair.

And Jewish tailors and shoemakers and tinsmiths
in wooden houses with shingled roofs.
Lived and worked day and night,
Jewish artisans, making a simple living...

Gentile peasants and women came into town
bringing fowl and corn and seeds
to Leyzer Buksnevsky and Meyer Yanusover
who dealt in grain, in flax and eggs.

In the shops and stalls that covered the market square
pins and needles and mirrors were sold,
buttons and beads to red-faced peasant girls
who'd been out guzzling beer with their menfolk.

Grune's hotel was well known
for its gefilte fish and its delicious pickles.
She delighted many a merchant and noble
who stopped in on their way back from the big city.

Drivers would rattle their wagons over the cobblestones.
Yude-Bereh-Lafer would yell curses their way,
a broom in his hand all day,
sweeping and sweeping after each horse went by.

***

Jewish peddlers would come around
on foot or with wagons over foot-paths and trails,
accompanied by the sun and the song of the corn
as they passed by decorated crosses on faraway roads.

There were no factories, just three mills
No large workshops, just one printing press
(Actually, there was one small plant
where Moshe Milner made seltzer and lemonade.)

But instead of the workshops or large factories
God hadn't neglected us; he provided

Green cucumbers
which were renowned over the whole nation.

Gentile women, from villages and town
From dawn to dusk, for two *lits* per day,
dug the earth and planted enough --
from Monday to Monday, working all the week long.

The priest would rail, the rabbi would preach
Sunday is sacred! You must keep Shabbat!
Addressing them like sheep who had wandered astray
A generation bent on sin, a world that is evil...

But half the town lives from this work
the entire summer long, and in winter, God bless!
They pickle the cucumbers and lay them away
with the stores of potatoes and cabbage.

And when winter's frosts fill up the roads,
when ice spreads over the Smilga and Neviazhe
the garden-keepers linger by the study house stove
while Kalmen the Pipe tells stories

of demons, thieves or even drunkards
who prey on Jews, causing grief
of spirits not long ago brought to the grave
that return from the river each Saturday night.

***

On the eve of Pesach the town felt renewed,
Jews in the town felt freer.
Jewish children were released from *cheder*
Jewish children played happily.

Houses were whitewashed, basements were scoured,
clean sand was spread over kitchen floors.
Pipes in the bathhouse hissed with steam
as people carried their matzos home.

Meyer Zaverukhe greased the wheels
of a carriage that had transported nobility
All winter long they had lain idle
while sleighs traveled over the snowy roads.

Modest maidens now blushed as they looked
at the young Jewish men they'd known as children
who now returned from the yeshivas of Telz or Slobodka
to enjoy the holiday in their home town.

The synagogue yard is full, *kennahora*, with Jews.
Jews head for afternoon prayers in the shul
wearing shoes instead of boots, new suits of clothes,
summer coats instead of fur wraps.

A clean hand towel hangs by the door
for holiday washing up.
Candlesticks, newly polished, give off bright light
and people's faces shine.

Windows opened, Jews take delight
in the breeze blowing into the study house.
It smells like spring, with the beloved holiday
with matzo, with mead and with Passover wine.

***

Thus Jews lived there for generations and years
Until one day a wicked official came riding in
from Kovno, the big city,
issuing many evil decrees

He made lists, wrote out orders,
drove the market out of the town center;
and in place of the brick market
installed a park...

And the priest in the church preached hatred:
"Jews, be damned and go to Palestine!"
And the assistant town-master was also unfriendly:
Day in, day out, he harassed the Jews.

The priest preached and the authorities incited:
"All the Jews' properties are all mortgaged,
the nobililty's impoverished, the gentiles are enslaved
Young Christian girls work as their servants!"

Hundreds of Jews, due to instability and poverty
leave the town, spreading all over the world.
People send their children off to strange lands:
To America, to Africa and also to Palestine.

The older generation is the one remaining.
The young have departed from there permanently.
Poverty has driven them away from the town
to find new homes across the sea.

***

But that Litvak town cannot be forgotten.
You've cut back on clothes, cut back on food,
exiled yourself to work among blacks on the Rand.
You were so green when you first arrived.

Everyone dreamt of those still in the town
while working hard from morning til night,
and of saving a little money after a few years
to bring the wife and children to Africa.

A society was founded here – people came together
to share all that was known about the folks back home.
Keidan still had an address: you could write
and hear of all the trouble and pain happening there.

Its children did not forget their home Keidan
They eased the burdens that oppressed the town:
Money and packages of food and clothing
and visas for relatives were sent.

We supported the synagogue, sent Passover charity
repaired the broken fence around the cemetery,
Sent young women there to find husbands
with trousseaus and dowries for their sisters...

And today the Lithuanian town still exists
with its Christian church, cemetery and cloister.
But Jews? In the town that calls itself Keidan?
There are no more Jews in Keidan!

Jewish property has been seized by gentiles.
Gentile families occupy Jewish houses.
The prayer-house doors are all boarded up
and Jewish children have dispersed.

An entire heroic community was brought low
in town by the Nazis, in the woods by starvation.
The gravestones stand witness
to the town's streets and fields.

There is no more Jewish Keidan in Lithuania.
Only its people remain to say *kaddish*
for its cruelly slaughtered residents.
Great is the tragedy, the wound is still fresh!

Copyright © Keidan Memorial Fund 2016
Translated by A Cassel.
Keidan Yizkor Book, pp. 299-306

Top: A section of Smilga Street, next to the well.

THE DESTRUCTION OF KEIDAN by *David Wolpe*

Originally published in the Yiddish journal, "Fun Letstn Khurbn" in Munich, 1948.

By June 24, within days after Germany launched its attack on the Soviet Union, Keidan was in German hands. Two months later, all that remained of the Jewish population there, was a large grave.

Only three Jewish eyewitnesses to the tragedy survived the dark Nazi period. These three men were later able to recount what happened there. I am here recording their words, and trying to reconstruct as accurately as possible the holocaust of the Jews of Keidan.

With the outbreak of the German-Russian war, there emerged in Keidan, as in other parts of Lithuania, the underground Lithuanian fifth column. Fascists and hooligans, realizing that the Nazi beast had broken loose and was on the march across the German-Lithuanian border, began organising themselves into the notorious Lithuanian "partisan" groups. Immediately preparations were made by them to receive their long awaited masters from the West. A leading part among the partisans was played by the professionals and the educated – by doctors, chemists, teachers, government officials, as well as their sons – the high school and university youths and pupils of the local Technicum and others. The Keidan "partisans" were headed by two notorious Lithuanians, Povylius and Markunas, both sons of past mayors in the time of the old fascist Lithuanian government. The three brothers Vacys, Juozas and Stepas Šulčas, who lived on the horse market square, were also leading members of the "partisans" of Keidan, and so was Vaclovas Lačinskas, a carpenter of Jasvener [Josvainių] Street. All these were particularly active in the murder and plunder of Jews.

The Jews of Keidan sensed that the atmosphere was charged with impending murder and pogrom. The good neighbours of the yesterday changed overnight. As time crept on, panic began mounting in Jewish homes. There was nobody to offer any advice or consolation. The Jews hid in their houses like hunted animals. Still, young people tried to flee and reach the Soviet lines, in order to enlist in the Russian army. They were shot at by Lithuanians, and a number were killed. Others were murdered on the roads by marauding Lithuanians. Only a small number managed to reach the Soviet lines and enlist in the army. Several won distinction in battle, and some died heroically on the battlefield, such as Izia Gladstein and others. An appreciable number of fleeing Jews came across the German army and had

Mr David Wolpe

David Wolpe, the writer of this article, is one of the young Hebrew-Yiddish writers and poets of Remnants of Jewry in Europe. Born in Keidan, David Wolpe went through all the horrors of the Ghettos and Concentration Camps. He spent a year in Dachau, and since his liberation he has been a regular contributor to all magazines of liberated Jewry in Germany. He is the editor of the magazine "Hemshech" ("Continuation") the organ of the Central Committee of the Remnant of Jewry in Germany. David Wolpe is the brother of Isaac Wolpe in Johannesburg, a member of the Committee of the Keidan Society. The two brothers met recently in Israel.

no alternative but to return to Keidan. One of them, a very gifted Jewish student, Nisan Zaltzburg, in desperation hanged himself on his return flight, in the nearby village of Shat.

As soon as the Germans entered Keidan they immediately decreed that all Jews should wear yellow patches. Jews were forbidden to walk on pavements or speak to Lithuanians. There were other, similar restrictions as well.

The first organised bloody action by Lithuanians was the rounding up of 100 Jews, alleged communists. They were marched in their underwear through the village and shot in the Babian (Borer) woods, about two miles from the town. The names known to me of those who were shot are: Beno Ronder; Gutman Bloomberg; Jacob Wolpert; Moishe Zalmanowitz with his two daughters Pesse and Bune; Polones the chemist; David Prusak; Avrohom Itche Dinershul; Shmulke the cab-driver (I cannot recollect his surname); and Jonah Shapiro.

A few more episodes from the first days of occupation: Meike Berger, a cinema owner, was beaten up so badly by Lithuanians that he died shortly after being taken to hospital. Reuven Chesler, a tailor, ran to his parents in "brom" (at the synagogue yard, where fowls used to be slaughtered) and was shot at the gate by a Lithuanian.

Keidener City Council in which Jews played a prominent part as can be seen in the above photograph, constituting 40 % of its members

A few days later Jews were driven to forced labour. The majority were employed at the airport, unpacking bombs left by the Russians. The guards were supplied by the newly formed Lithuanian police. Lithuanian civilians watched from a distance to gloat over the misery of the Jews. Some bombs exploded and about ten Jews were killed.

Other Jews worked in the neighbouring government estates, such as Pelednagiai (where in the 1920s the first *hachshara* [Zionist training] farm in Lithuania was established), Podborok, Zherginiai, and others.

Jewish girls were taken to the German officers' club where they were criminally assaulted.

The brutal tortures and murder continued unabated and the Jews lived in constant terror of what the next day might bring.

On July 23rd, Lithuanians, with the assistance of a few Germans, loaded some 200 Jews on six trucks, allegedly to transport them to their labour destinations. After the Jews failed to return, members of their families endeavoured to learn of their fates from Lithuanian leaders, but to no avail. A Lithuanian was later bribed with a large sum of money and he brought them the news that on the very same day (July 23) all 200 were shot in the Tevtshunai woods, 10 miles from Keidan. The Jews of Keidan did not want to believe the story, and hoped that their nearest and dearest would still return. When a good few days had passed, however, they realized that the news was authentic.

Among these 200 were: Israel Kahn and his three sons, Zalman, Feivl and Ortchik; Ortchik Karnowsky, who lived near the horse market; the two butcher brothers, Yankl and Leizer together with Leizer's son Bine; the chemist Kagan and his brother-in-law the hardware merchant Pruzhansky; Israel Toiber the baker, with his wife and little daughter; Mina Shilkiner who had a stall at the market.

Shortly after the above event, the Mayor of Keidan, Povylius (who had been reinstated to his former post by the Germans) summoned the leading Jews of Keidan: Tzadok Shlapobersky, Chaim Ronder, Chaim Blumberg, Abrasha Kagan, Sroelov, Sholem Chait and others. Povylius informed them that within twenty-four hours all Jews must leave their homes and move into the vicinity of Smilga Street. Smilga Street, together with the synagogue, the synagogue-yard and the neighbouring alleys up to Langer [Gedimino] Street were fenced off by a barbed wire fence, and this became the ghetto of Keidan.

On the day the Jews moved into the ghetto, the Lithuanians brought to Keidan all the Jews of the neighbouring villages of Shat and Zheim, all in all about a thousand people. Among them were also the Jews of other nearby villages, who had fled to Shat and Zheim at the outbreak of war. The overcrowding in the ghetto of Keidan became unbearable. In addition the food supplies of almost everybody were exhausted. Famine and typhus were imminent.

Jewish Firemen played a prominent part in the Keidan Brigade

Keidan Jewish High School

Members of the Hashomer Hatzair group

A group of Jewish Orphans. The Jewish Orphanage was one of many institutions destroyed by the Nazis

The mayor imposed a tax on the Jews and threatened extermination unless the required amount became available. The Jews of Keidan gathered all their jewellery and money and gave whatever they could lay their hands on, in the hope that that might improve their lot. The hoped-for improvement did not come about. The Jews of Keidan were forced within a short period to contribute taxes on several other occasions.

Some of the youth of Keidan realized the desperate situation and urged leading Jews to flee and hide in the woods or elsewhere. The community leaders, however, were opposed to such a step. They thought that it would endanger the whole ghetto. They were under the impression that all the Germans wanted was Jewish labour, and it was therefore unwise to risk one's life.

August 15 put an end to all illusions and hopes. On this day, Lithuanian police and "partisans," under the command of a few Germans, drove all Jews from their homes into the synagogue-yard. All men over the age of fourteen were marched off four abreast to the huge brick stables of Zhirgynas in the park, which had been a stud farm. The women and children, the old and the ailing were packed on carts and carted away. Even women with newborn babies were ordered out of the hospital and brought to the yard. The Lithuanian intelligentsia flocked to witness the spectacle as if it were a circus. Zhirgynas, where the Jewish men were taken, was heavily guarded by Lithuanians. The Jews were kept there for thirteen days. The stables were terribly overcrowded and with the exception of coffee, the Jews received no food at all. The Lithuanians paid the prisoners a few visits and divested them of anything they may still have had left.

When the Jews were driven from the ghetto to the synagogue-yard, Benzy Birger suggested to a few of the younger ones that they should try and escape past the Smilga creek. Not finding any adherents to his plan, he himself fled. For days he hid in the bush. Later, from a hiding place he witnessed executions of Jews. After the slaughter he went to some peasant friends (he was a farmer) and was hidden by them. He survived the Nazis and lives at present in Keidan.

Yiddish Folk School, Keidan

Scene of a play produced by the Yiddish Folk School

On Thursday, August 28, 1941, about 200 Lithuanians assembled at Zhirgynas. They were railway workers and police, all armed with rifles and hand grenades. First the young and strong Jews were separated, grouped in batches of sixty and taken behind the Catholic cemetery, close to Dotnuva Road, near the Smilga creek. (The Jewish cemetery is higher on a hill above the creek.) There a huge pit was ready which had taken Russian prisoners of war five days to dig. The Jews were forced to strip at the mouth of this pit, and the Lithuanians directed machine guns at them. At the time of this shooting, tractor motors were started in order to silence the shrieks of horror which could even be heard in Keidan. Many wounded fell into this grave, and a number who had not been hit were pushed in and buried alive. This spectacle was watched by prominent members of Lithuanian society of Keidan, such as the principal of the high school, Selava, the Mayor Povylius, and the young Catholic priest was also present.

Rabbi Aaron Galin (the son-in-law of the Rabbi of Keidan, Reb Shlomo Feinsilber), Chairman of the Rabbinical Association of Lithuania, who was also in Zhirgynas, was among the first batch. Standing at the pit he addressed the Jews. He said that the Jewish people had already experienced a great many trials. When he cried that "the innocent blood of those murdered will not remain silent" the shooting commenced.

During the execution there were attempts at fighting back. Among the second batch was Tzadok Shlapobersky, a man of about forty. He had been an officer in the Lithuanian army and had taken part in the fight for Lithuania's liberation. He had also been a city councillor for many years and was friendly with the Lithuanians. A German officer was in charge of the massacre. Shlapobersky asked to say a few words. The German started to beat him. Shlapobersky grabbed the German, pulled him into the pit and began strangling him. A Lithuanian with an automatic rifle who stood nearby immediately jumped to the German's assistance. His name was Raudonis, the owner of the Hotel Vilnius in the building of the Jewish photographer Joffe. Shlapobersky let the German go, jumped on the Lithuanian and bit his throat. Shlapobersky was pierced by the bayonets of other Lithuanians and his body was cut to shreds. The gasping Raudonis was immediately taken to hospital where he died two days later. The Lithuanians accorded him an imposing funeral. A number of enthusiastic addresses were held in which the Lithuanian bandit was described as "the last victim of Jewish power."

After Shlapobersky's heroic death, the murders became more brutal but also more cautious. The Nazis led smaller groups of Jews to the pit.

In one of the groups there was the locksmith, Boruch Meir Chesler, the proprietor of a radio and cycle store and locksmith shop. At the pit he wrenched an automatic pistol from the hands of a Lithuanian, but unfortunately he did not know how to use it. At the same moment, two boys fled toward the creek, but they as well as Chesler were shot dead.

The men were followed by women and bigger children, in batches of forty. The blood-thirst of the murderers kept on mounting. Rachel Shisiansky, the wife of Aba Shisiansky, the miller, pleaded that she be shot first before her children, whereupon the children were wrenched from her and shot before her eyes, and only then did the beasts shoot her. The elderly and ailing women were brought in cars and were buried alive. The small children were thrown like balls in the air by Lithuanians and caught on the bayonets.

Lithuanians of Keidan related later that after the pit was covered with a bit of earth, the surface heaved up and down as if a live pulse was pulsating in the mass grave, and blood seeped through to the surface. The murderers used rollers to press the earth down in order to arrest the heaving of the bloody earth made alive.

Jews of Keidan who visited the mass grave after liberation stated that the square grave remained higher than the surrounding surface, as if the holy grave wished to separate from the unclean soil which surrounds it.

The shooting of the Jews continued until the evening.

Fearing the bitter end that was in store for him, the butcher Hirsh Levyotkin hanged himself while still in Zhirgynas.

Of all the Jews who were locked up in Zhirgynas, only two escaped by some miracle: Chaim Ronder, born in Keidan in 1903, and Shmuel Smolsky, born in Posen, a refugee who fled Poland in 1939 and settled in Keidan. Ronder and Smolsky hid themselves behind planks which were lying in Zhirgynas. The clothing of the murdered Jews was brought to Zhirgynas after the slaughter and the place was guarded. The best items of clothing were plundered by the leaders of the mass murder. The remaining clothes were sorted and later sold cheaply to the Lithuanian population. On the same night of the massacre the two Jews, who lay hidden behind the planks and under piles of clothing, used a penknife to carve a hole in the shingled roof of the stable, took off their boots and lowered themselves on a rope made from torn sheets. Luckily they were not seen by the guards and succeeded in reaching the Podborik wood.

Thus, together with the above-mentioned Benzy Birger, of the 4,000 martyrs of the three Jewish congregations of Keidan, Shat and Zheim, only three Jews survived.

Copyright © Keidan Memorial Fund 2016

IN MEMORIAM

Moshe and Chayeh Liebeh Volpe A'H murdered by the Nazis in Keidan

Communal Buildings Destroyed by the Nazis

1 The shul grounds in which the Beit HaMedrash and the Shul are visible. In the forefront is the portal together with the abattoir.

2 The Jewish Peoples' Bank assisted merchants and labourers with the required loans.
The lettering on the facade of the building Yiddishe Folksbank

3 The Beit HaMedrash on the other side of the water and
4 The hand carved Aron Kodesh (Holy Ark) in the Keidaner Shul was renowned for its artistic beauty.

3 The wooden synagogue – "the Soldiers' Kloyz.   *4 A hand-made work of art in wood.*

5 The small shul on Smilger Street.

6 The Old Beit HaMedrash in Keidan : In a letter, recently received, it was reported that the doors and windows had been boarded up with planks.

7 The Big Shul where they only prayed in the summertime.

AMONG THE RUINS *by Chaim Ronder*

This letter was sent to the Keidaner Society of Johannesburg by Chaim Ronder, a partisan during the period of occupation.

POGEGEN (Pagėgiai) 7 November, 1946

Warm brotherly greetings to you, Jews of Johannesburg – born in what was Keidan. Yes, what *was* Keidan, because Keidan no longer exists for us. The cobblestones of Keidan are soaked in blood and tears, and each time I pass Keidan, I see in my imagination, from the side of the Dotnuva Road, in a pit 90 metres long, 3 metres wide and 3 metres deep, our mothers, fathers and our little babies, weeping and crying. It seems to me as if they are pleading: "Open this grave and let us see how our enemies look today. The commander who led us to the slaughter, and – after Tzadok Shlapobersky wounded him by the pit and fell as a hero – shouted 'You leprous dogs, you infected the whole of Europe!' – how does he look today?"

And at the same time, I think: "Yes, you innocent souls, what a pity that you cannot rise from your grave. You would take great satisfaction to see how our enemy looks today. You could take revenge on the bloodthirsty dogs, just as I am taking revenge. You would see how they are rebuilding our ruined towns and villages, how they are reopening mass graves in the Slabodka ghetto and transferring the bodies to the Jewish cemetery. You would go through East Prussia and see entire districts without Germans. You would see a sign at the entrance to Tilsit that says "Sovetsk City" and one at Koenigsberg labeled "Kaliningrad," because Tilsit and Koenigsberg no longer exist. Their names and memories were destroyed by the heroic Red Army. The filthy Prussian military boot is gone forever. You would see all this and take great pleasure in it, as I do, but… unfortunately, this is impossible. Our sorrow is too great. The heart grieves and aches to think of times gone by.

My dear friend Chaim, I received your first letter along with your parcels. You ask me to let you know about your family. Indeed, brother, what can I write you? Their fate was the same as everyone's. I understand you and all our brethren abroad. No one wants to believe. Only those who lived through all this can believe. Unfortunately, I am the only one who remained alive and has seen everything. Your brothers, David, Benjamin, and your brother-in-law Yudl Shteinbach slept next to me the last night, on bags of oats. I pleaded with Benjamin, "Let's run away," but he answered, "I don't believe, they will not shoot, and secondly, where will you run to? There is no place."

Indeed, his second answer, that there was no place to run, was correct. If I could but tell you what I experienced during those three years… But that is impossible, no one can describe it and no one would believe it. More than once did I swim rivers in strange places, under a hail of bullets. There was a reward of 20,000 marks on my head but they never caught me. On the contrary, with a weapon in my hand, I brought some of them down and I'm still taking revenge today. In truth I am ill from three years of wandering in the forests, yet my revenge continues.

Dear Chaim, write and tell me where is your brother Zalman, with whom I studied in *cheder*. Where are Velvke Shilkeiner, Mendel Sadovsky and the other Keidaners? Write to me, all of you, because you cannot imagine how precious is each word from you for somebody who remained completely alone.

My dear Jewish brothers, forgive me for answering you all in one letter, but I believe you will all meet to read this together. Indeed, I cannot reply to each one individually, because you are many and I am one. But please, write me, each one separately, because a few words from each of you brings us consolation, especially as we are so alone here.

I received a letter from Itzik Setting's son, asking about the fate of his family. Sadly, I must answer that his father, mother and sister were killed on 28 August 1941, together with all the other Jews. They were buried in the same 90-metre mass grave. His brother-in-law Yeshayahu Eides was killed with a group of 225[1] Jews in the first days after the Germans marched into Keidan. I don't remember the exact date, but I more or less remember that the following Jews were shot to death then in the Borer [Babeniai] woods:

Moshe Zalmanowitz and his two daughters; Tuvya Jaffe and his son; Shmuel Abramowitz (Leizer Elye's son-in-law); my cousin Benjamin Ronder; Faivel Friedland; Gedalia Berzak; Dovidke Michaels; Shmuel Berger (the coachman). Dovid Michaels was badly tortured. They flogged him until he was half dead, then poured water on him and beat him again until he expired. The manager of the Peoples' Bank, Kuldenitsky, and many others, whose names I can't recall.

---

[1] Other sources put the number shot at Babenai at 125, including Jews and others.

And now, dear Beyla Kagan (Morgenshtern), I received your letter. Unfortunately I cannot bring you good news with my reply. The fate of your family is identical to that of all the others. I can only tell you a few details about your brother, Efraim. On 15 August 1941, Saturday, at 7 in the morning, all of us, inhabitants of Keidan, were driven out of our houses and forbidden to take anything with us. Old and young, big and small, mothers with babies in their arms were all brought to the synagogue yard. There they lined us up in rows of four and marched us through Smilga Street to the Keidan courtyard.[2] German and Lithuanian policemen, armed with submachine guns and automatic weapons, walked alongside. I was in the first rows, together with your brother, Efraim. We all wore yellow Stars of David, one on the chest and another on the back....

The sight and the atmosphere were terrifying. They locked us in a large warehouse there, 3,700 people. Together with us they brought Jews from Shat and Zheim [Šėta and Žeimiai]. There was no place to lie down, or even space to stand. We remained in these conditions until the day of the massacre, August 28. On August 26, Hirshel Levyotkin was found hanging in that same warehouse, among some carts. He was still warm when we took him down from the gallows. I, your brother Efraim, Moshe Levyotkin, David Geben and Tzadok Shlapobersky brought him to the Jewish cemetery and buried him.

When we left the cemetery, its new owner, a farmer named Stankiewicz, whom I took out after I was liberated, demanded that we pay for the wooden planks, which belonged to us. We paid him 100 marks and together all burst into tears like little children, realizing that even old acquaintances wanted our blood. I never saw Efraim again after that. Indeed, Beylinka, in your letter you remind me of how I used to come on horseback and similar memories from our younger days. You mention Basha Ronder, with her friendly greetings — but what can we do, they are no more. All that remains is a ghastly pit, dark and long, which we have fenced in with steel wire.

Abrasha Kagan kissed me ten minutes before his death and cried, saying: "Never mind, our blood will be avenged." He didn't lie. Vengeance has come and how deep is my joy that I participated, and I am still taking part to this day.

Berl, why have you not written a few words? Believe me, because I feel so lonely, every word of yours brings comfort. When I receive a letter from abroad, from any one of you, my heart swells and my eyes fill with tears of joy. Because, as I have written before: Keidan no longer exists and you are its only remnants. So, every word from you brings consolation.

Ten days ago I was in Vilna, at Guta Kagan's. I stayed over with her for six nights. She is the only friend left with whom I can share memories. Berl, may I trouble you to find, in Johannesburg or elsewhere, my two cousins, Aba Ronder and Gavriel Ronder. Please give them my address and ask them to write to me.

In 1944, four months after my liberation, I received a telegram from the Keidan Jews in Africa, with the following contents: "As we have been informed that you have survived, we ask you to send us the names of the Jews of Keidan who remained alive. Then we will send urgent help." Unfortunately, there was no return address, so I couldn't contact you.

A few days later, I received a second telegram, from Aba Ronder, asking about his sister, Hirsh Golombek's wife. I replied and never heard from him again. Let him know that his sister was killed in Keidan together with all the Jews. His sister-in-law, Sarah Ronder from Shavl [Šiauliai] is alive. She returned from the Stutthof camp in Germany, her two children perished in the death camp. Also his relatives, the Brett family from Shadove [Šeduva] remained alive. Please, look for him and ask him to contact us. We are together in Pogegen [Pagėgiai], also my cousin Velveh Ronder's youngest son, who returned from the battlefront, is here. Where is David Rappoport? If he is in Johannesburg, he should write to me. He was one of my best friends from childhood.

I must dedicate a special account of those sad days to Tzadok Shlapobersky. His name sets an example of bravery, for me and for all of us. He has entered the annals of history of the Jews of Keidan. Hirsh Shlapobersky, be comforted that your brother Tzadok was the one who in the last minutes before his death, dragged the German commander into the pit and injured him. At that moment, the shooting stopped and policemen, wanting to save the commander, jumped into the pit with their bayonets. A life-and-death struggle followed. As a result, Tzadok bit the throat of one of the policemen, who fell like a dog on the spot. He also injured a second policeman, who died a few days later. Because of this, they stabbed Tzadok with their bayonets till his body became like a sieve. He was the only one who died as a hero and took vengeance on the bloodthirsty dogs. On August 28 you should at least be consoled by your brother's bravery. I personally will never forget him, since he was one of my best friends, if not the best of them.

---

[2] This likely refers to the Zhirgynas stables outside Keidan.

And now about your sister Rashel. In February 1945 I was in Kovno for a few days. Suddenly I learned that in the region of East Prussia that had been taken by the heroic Red Army, a few hundred women had been liberated, of whom 13 had reached Kovno and among them was a woman from Keidan, named Shlapobersky. I searched half a day until I found her. I have no words to describe how she looked. Wearing a flimsy dress, with a yellow star of David on her back, she was completely swollen, her hands and feet frozen. We both burst into tears because she was the first and the only woman from Keidan who had returned from the hell of the camps. Weak and hungry, she was unable to walk. I quickly got her a fur coat and felt boots and brought her to Keidan by car. There I arranged a place for her with a Christian acquaintance. I took care of her and gave her medicine.

At this same time, I received a letter from a young man from Krekinava, who had returned from the battlefront (his family name was Peipert). He wrote that he had found a Jewish girl living with a Christian man, who said she was the daughter of Eliyahu Shlapobersky from Keidan. I helped Rashel as much as I could until April 16, when I left for East Prussia. She is presently in Vilna, bringing up Eliyahu's daughter.

And now, about your brother, Eliyahu Shlapobersky. It is known that he lived in Kovno and was in the Kovno ghetto until 1943. In 1943, the Germans transferred 500 Jews from the Kovno ghetto, men and women, to Keidan and established a camp for them. Among these were Gurvitz the pharmacist's two daughters Mina and Zhenia, and your brother Eliyahu. I was then in a partisan unit which was fighting in the area of Keidan, Jonava, Kovno and Vilkomir [Ukmergė]. When I heard that a Jewish camp had been established in Keidan and that Eliyahu was there, I contacted them, with great difficulty. We secretly sent them weapons and in November 1943 I went with a group of fifteen people to the Keidan airfield. We crossed to the Borer woods in small boats, attacked the guards in the middle of the night and brought out 25 Jews. During the action, two Jews from the camp were killed along with three partisans and four Germans. We didn't manage to achieve any more than this, as we would all have been killed if we tried.

From the liberated Jews I learned that Eliyahu had been sent back two weeks earlier to the Kovno ghetto, where he perished when the Germans set the ghetto on fire as they retreated. So, dear Hirsh, you have an exact picture from a living witness who saw all this.

I think that this is enough for today, because if I wanted to describe for you everything that I have experienced, there wouldn't be enough paper and ink. Also, the nerves wouldn't allow it. I began writing this letter at nine in the evening, and it is already four in the morning.

Dear Chaim, Berl, Beyla and other friends from the former Keidan, write to me, each of you separately, and I will answer you all together. I would like to know details about everyone, since I studied in cheder with many of you. How good it was then! And today? Alone, broken, the souls of our family members who were killed are in front of me always.

Today we celebrated the great holiday of the October Revolution. Thanks to the mighty Red Army, we remain alive and continue to exist, in defiance of all our enemies. And if the dark forces of reaction try again, their fingers will be burnt, because we are the victors. We fought for a just cause, and the Goerings, Streichers, Rosenbergs and their followers are now swinging from the gallows. Those who have not yet been hanged, will be strung up — may their names and memories be obliterated.

Dear brothers, I end my letter and wish you all a good future.

Your brother and friend, Chaim Ronder.

I'd also like to ask the Jews from the older generation to write to me. We don't know each other but they knew my father and they remember Yudl Ronder when he was in Africa. Are Pesach Stein and Chana Shayevich in Johannesburg? I studied in cheder with them.

My address:

Lithuanian SSR,
District Department of the Commisariat of the Internal Affairs,
Pogegen Town,
Ronder Chaim Yudelevich.

Keidan Yizkor Book pp 286-290

Copyright © Keidan Memorial Fund 2016

GOLDEN JUBILEE OF THE KEIDAN HELPING HAND AND BENEVOLENT SOCIETY IN JOHANNESBURG

Jewish emigration from Keidan to South Africa began as far back as before the Boer War, and at the turn of the century several immigrants from Keidan could already be found both in Cape Town and in Johannesburg. Finding themselves in a strange country they felt the need of getting together in order to share their memories of the old home as well as their experiences in the new country.

The first immigrants from Keidan dreamt of forming a society of mutual aid of Keidan Landsleit. In 1900 it was finally decided to form such a society in Johannesburg. Owing to conditions prevailing in Johannesburg at the time as a result of the Boer War, it was resolved to postpone the official establishment of the society until after the war. The Society was officially inaugurated in 1903 and was known as the Keidan Benevolent Society. The main object of the Society in those days was mainly to render medical assistance to those members who required it. Membership was open to all born in Keidan or vicinity, to those whose wives had been born in Keidan or neighbourhood as well as to all those who lived in Keidan for at least a year before their departure for South Africa. Members were expected to visit sick Landsleit at the request of the Committee.

The first Committee of the Keidan Society consisted of:

Zwi Hirsh Traub
Chayim Crost
Ben Zion Traivish
Abraham Abe Levitan
Joshua Shaiowitz
Zemach Wolpe
Nathan Kramer
Aharon Goldberg
Wolf Ronder
Chayim Moishe Denebursky

Unfortunately today none of the members of the original Committee are alive, and when we celebrate the Golden Jubilee of our Society we must pay tribute to the memory of the first pioneers from Keidan who founded the Keidan Society, and thus established an organisation which not only assisted hundreds of Landsleit to establish themselves in the new country but also contributed greatly towards organised Jewish life in South Africa.

The late Mr and Mrs Isaac Cohen were among the foundation members of the Society.

The following foundation members of the Keidan Society of 50 years ago are still among us today: H Schlapobersky, L Shilaner, N Brener, B Elk, Wolf (the eldest son of Itzik Yechiel), and we extend our heartiest congratulations to them on the occasion of our celebrations.

The first immigrants from Keidan, as most of the immigrants from Lithuania, reached South Africa without their families were either single or married men who had left their families behind in the old home. They were lonely and homeless and clung to one another. They felt like brothers and shared their joys and sorrows. The Society helped them to strike roots in the new difficult surroundings away from the homes where they had been brought up and from a Jewish life to which they were accustomed. The Society eased their feeling of loneliness and homelessness and created an atmosphere of the old home in the new surroundings.

Members of the society met frequently in a closely knit circle. Every member showed deep concern for the welfare and well-being of the other landsleit.

On April 24th, 1904, the Constitution of the Society was adopted, which defined the duties and privileges of members as well as of the Committee. At the time of its foundation the society numbered 40 members.

During the first World War, the Society assisted its Landsleit in the old home, and when the Jews of Keidan returned to their home town from the various places to which they had been driven by the Czarist regime, the Keidan Society here in South Africa assisted them financially.

In 1916 the Society established a Gemilus Chasodim Loan Fund and the Society became known as the Keidan Helping Hand and Benevolent Society. With the foundation of the Loan Fund the activities of the Society greatly expanded and a specific Fund was created by means of special contributions received from members. An annual Purim Ball was held, the proceeds of which were devoted to the Loan Fund. It was with the aid of loans advanced by the Society that a number of Keidan Landsleit succeeded in getting established in business and trade. They were thus enabled to either assist their families in Keidan or bring them out to South Africa. The loans advanced were between £25 - £30 and were granted to needy members without any difficulty or unpleasantness.

On June 2, 1916, the Committee confirmed the bye-laws of the Loan Fund Society. The Committee consisted of: Mr Schlapobersky, Chairman, M Rosenberg, Vice-Chairman, B Elk, Treasurer, and the following members: M Weitzer, I Markunsky, A Dangel and A Licker. M Linde was the Hon Secretary.

For a certain period the Society had its own Minyan during the High Festivals and acquired its own Sefer Torah. The Minyan was held either at the Palmerston Hotel or in Balmoral Chambers. The income thus derived was devoted to the funds of the Society. Later their Sefer Torah was handed to the Braamfontein Synagogue.

After the First World War, a great number of immigrants began arriving in South Africa. Among them there were many from Keidan. The society grew both in membership and in the scope of its activities. The society assisted a number of the newly arrived immigrants financially and helped them to establish themselves. Thanks to the Helping Hand Society a great number of immigrants established businesses or obtained employment, and it is gratifying to note that many of them were most successful in their undertakings. The new arrivals took an active part in the work of the Society which increased its contributions to the old home. In those days of Jewish autonomy in Lithuania, a number of Jewish national and communal institutions were established in Keidan, and the Keidan Society of Johannesburg assisted them financially.

The members of the society took an active part in the "War Victims Fund" which conducted a drive for funds for Jewish war victims in Eastern Europe. The leaders of the Society took a prominent part in the conduct of the campaign.

With the introduction of the Quota Laws in South Africa in 1930, emigration from Lithuania into South Africa was brought to a standstill and almost no new immigrants arrived. The Society, however, continued with its activities of helping Landsleit in South Africa and assisting Jewish institutions in Keidan.

The position of the Jews in Lithuania deteriorated gradually, particularly in the economic field and more and more of our friends in the old home had to fall back on help from South Africa.

The terrible tragedy which befell European Jewry during the Second World War did not pass by our old and beloved Jewish community of Keidan, which was destroyed, together with the rest of Lithuanian Jewry. Only a few Landsleit survived the Nazi blood bath. In 1944, the Keidan Society inaugurated the "Keidan and District Relief Fund", which immediately upon its inception commenced to render assistance to surviving Landsleit who were either scattered all over Russia or languished in the camps of Germany and Italy. The Society endeavoured to obtain the names and addresses of all surviving landsleit in order to be in a position to help them. Some 120 such names were received and the Society began to despatch regular monthly parcels of food and clothing to them. The majority of these landsleit are at present in Israel and the Society keeps in touch with them. The Society, for instance helped a young man from Keidan who was suffering from tuberculosis to undergo a course of treatment in Switzerland and maintained him throughout his treatment. It is gratifying to learn that this young man is at present in Israel where he qualified as an electrician.

The Relief Fund was registered in 1944 with the Welfare Board as a welfare society, which enabled us to embark upon fund raising ventures in a more efficient and organised manner. Our Society was the first and only one of all Landsmanshaften to be thus registered. This enhanced our prestige in the Jewish community.

A most important achievement of our Society which is also unique among such societies was the formation of a company known as "Keidan Settlement, Ltd.," This Company has been registered with an appreciable capital for the purpose of building homes in Israel for Keidan Refugees. Our late lamented Landsman, Samuel Stein, subscribed an amount of £5,000 for the objects of the company.

COMMITTEE AND MEMBERS OF THE KEIDAN SOCIETY

Front row: (from left to right – Messrs H Taub, Ralph Rabinowitz, and L.Nevsky, Middle row-Messrs H Schlapobersky, S Keidan, A Levin, M Stein (Chairman Keidan Relief Fund), B Krost (Chairman Keidan Society). M Cohen and I Wolpe. Back row – Messrs Ch Geben, N Berger, M Rochin, S Kaplan, I Krost, M Minsk, Ch Dangel and J Goldberg.

Representatives of the Society, among them the late Mr Samuel Stein, and the Committee members, Messrs S Keidan and I Wolpe, visited Israel and negotiated with the Directors of the JNF the setting aside of a suitable piece of ground near Tel Aviv for the building of homes for refugees from Keidan.

We hope that it will not be long before we are in a position to commence building operations, and thus our Society will not only play its part in a work of help, and rehabilitation for our Landsleit in Israel, which will be a source of pride to us, but will also make its contribution in the up building of Israel. The Keidan Society undertook to bear the expenditure involved in the building of a reading hall and library in the Kibbutz "Beit Zera", where a number of families hailing from Keidan are concentrated. This hall will serve as a Memorial to Keidan and will house documents, books and pictures dealing with Jewish Keidan. On the anniversaries of the destruction of Keidan Jewry, all Keidan landsleit in Israel will assemble in this hall in order to commemorate their brethren – the martyrs of Keidan. This structure will be a fitting, though modest, way of perpetuating the memory of the important spiritual Jewish centre of Keidan which no longer exists.

The fiftieth anniversary of the activities of the Keidan Society coincides with half a century of Jewish life in Johannesburg. It must be mentioned that members of the Keidan Society have taken an active part in all spheres of Jewish endeavour in Johannesburg. In general members of our Society played their part in the development of Johannesburg. Members of the Keidan Society have left their mark in the building industry, and many imposing structures in the Golden City were built by our members. Apart from the contributions of the late Samuel Stein who built a

COMMITTEE AND MEMBERS OF THE KEIDAN LADIES' SOCIETY

Front Row: (sitting from left to right)- Mesdames E G Shilainer, S Cohen, S Lipchik, G Rochin and H Geben. Back Row: (standing)- Mesdames M Gordon, Ch Goldberg, T Wolpe, E Krost, Ch Dangel, B Kaplan, M Charnass, R Oseia.

number of magnificent buildings in Johannesburg, other members of the Society also contributed their share to the growth of Johannesburg and its changing skyline.

Members of the Keidan Society participated in the activities of all Jewish organisations in Johannesburg. The Society has been affiliated to the SA Jewish Board of Deputies since the board's inception, and Mr H Schlapobersky has represented the Society on the Board throughout all these years. Our members have participated in all campaigns and drives held in Johannesburg for local and national causes and institutions.

The women's Keidan Society was founded after the First World War. Among the foundation members were Mesdames Brener, Hershovits, Wolpe, Weitzer, Werksman, Feinberg, Stein and Shilaner.

The Women's Society took an active part in the Relief Campaigns and organised a number of functions in order to raise funds for needy landsleit in the old home. The Women greatly assisted in the annual Passover Relief Drives. The women's Society helped a great deal in Drives for funds for the Keidan survivors of Nazi brutality. They sent a number of parcels frequently and regularly to their unfortunate brethren wherever they were.

On the occasion of the celebration of the Fiftieth Anniversary of our Society we must not forget that this joyous event is mixed with sadness. We celebrate the Fiftieth Anniversary of our Society at a time when Jewish Keidan, which boasted of a Jewish past of five hundred years, is no longer there, but was brutally wiped out by forces of darkness. We cannot forget Jewish Keidan, which was a centre of Torah and Culture in Jewish Lithuania. We have received numerous messages of congratulation from various bodies on the occasion of our celebration but there was no message from Jewish Keidan, which is, alas no more in existence.

During our festivities we must remember our martyrs, who together with millions of other Jews were so cruelly and brutally murdered by the Nazis. We must remember that we can perpetuate their memories in a corner of Israel, as we intend doing, and we must endeavour and remain true to the traditions of the Jews of Keidan who cherished and revered Jewish values and our spiritual heritage.

Let the glorious memory of the Jewish community of Keidan with its rich and wonderful past shine upon our festivities and may it lead us towards further fruitful and devoted activity for the welfare of our people.

Parents, brothers and sisters of Mr A Levin

Reb Chayim Moshe Denebursky A"H   Avrohom Abba Levitan
Two of the founders of the Keidaner Society.

The Organising Committee of the Jubilee Ball :
Seated: (Left to right) B Krost, A Levin (Chairman of the Organising Committee), M Shtein, M Cohen and Y Volpe
Standing: Max Rochin, H Shlapobersky, S Keidan and Ch Geben (Secretary)

THE KEIDANER ASSOCIATION IN SOUTH AFRICA by *Max Rochin*

After World War I, immediately after the liberation of Lithuania, the Lithuanian government granted the Jews a certain autonomy. A Jewish National Council was set up, yet all this lasted only a short time.

The situation in Lithuania as well as in Keidan deteriorated; there was no employment and no sources of income for people. A big emigration began. People would go to any place in the world. Many young people went to Palestine, many went to South America and many left for South Africa.

Those who went to South Africa and had no relatives in the foreign country, could address themselves to the Keidaner Society with all their problems. The Society took an interest in the problems of each one, helped some of them getting work, assisted others with a loan and arranged for them a livelihood, others received tools and even loans in order to support the wife and the family left behind in Keidan. Medical assistance and medicaments were given to all free of charge, and in this way everyone arranged himself gradually.

In course of time the Society increased, because new townspeople arrived, yet the more townspeople came, the more the situation of the Society became difficult, as it became necessary to help each one and there were no funds. As soon as one person finished to pay his loan, another one applied for help, and the members of the committee had big difficulties in satisfying everybody.

Every Sunday the members of the committee used to go and collect the membership fees, two shillings and six pence a month, and on Monday at the meeting each of them brought with him the money. After the collected money was summed up at the meeting, there was a great joy: it will be possible to pay the doctor, the pharmacy and it will be possible to grant the most urgent loan which an immigrant is already expecting for so long.

At the beginning of 1930 many townspeople came, because in May the immigration was stopped and no more immigrants came from Lithuania and Keidan. The Society had at that time very big difficulties in helping everybody to arrange themselves. The situation in Keidan deteriorated, each one received letters from his father, mother, brothers and sisters with pleas to save them and to send them help. Different institutions wrote to the Society too, that they perish, because the population cannot maintain them. So, for instance, the public bath was burnt and the town remained without a bath. Meetings were arranged but there were no means to rebuild the bath. We held immediately a meeting of all the townspeople and the necessary sum was collected.

Or a public appeal – there was a big flood which destroyed amongst other things the fence of the cemetery, and it is necessary to fortify the hill, otherwise the graves will collapse and the Chevra Kadisha has no money. We had to save and send money. We collected again the necessary funds and sent it to Keidan.

Again a request, – the roof of the big synagogue is decayed and it rains into it, the Scrolls of the Law and the holy books are being damaged. We collected the money and sent it to Keidan.

The town became poor and together with it the people. When Passover approached, there was no possibility to collect "Maot Chitin." Again they appealed to us. Unfortunately there was no unity between the public workers of Keidan. There were two institutions. One of these was the Kehila and the other one — "Ezra," and both of them appealed, and we didn't know what to do. The result was that we sent to both institutions and they distributed according to their understanding.

We used to organise two campaigns every year, one for winter to buy timber and the other one for "Maot Chitin[3]," and we continued so till the big destruction of the world, which befell the humanity and our beloved Keidan.

During World War II the situation changed completely. Keidan was unfortunately closed and we heard no more from there. Here in South Africa, the townspeople already were a little established, some more some less. We continued with our work. Some of our people still needed loans, and we continued with our system of doctor and medicaments. We also used to come to meetings. We were thinking only about the fate of the Jews in Keidan. During the war we believed that when the war comes to an end, we shall be able again to rebuild Keidan. We began collecting money by different means and we raised a big sum.

Unfortunately there was already no need for funds in Keidan. There were found only a few townspeople in the DP camps in Germany or dispersed all over Russia and in Vilnius. We found all our townspeople and assisted them with hundreds of packages of food and clothing. Our women worked around the clock and they packed and mailed till the camps in Germany became empty, thanks to the State of

---
[3] Charity distributed at Passover

Israel, where the majority of our townspeople lives today.

We also assisted our townspeople in Israel. We established a loan fund in Israel, which the townspeople in Israel use to their best.

Many townspeople still remained all over Russia and we mailed to them packages and clothing as well as different useful articles, till approximately 1970, when we became informed that they had troubles from the government and we stopped mailing packages to them.

Recently we sent aid to the new immigrants from Russia and we participated in the Memorial Book, which will be an eternal monument for our Keidan.

Copyright © Keidan Memorial Fund 2016

Top: The bridge over the Neviazhe (Nevėžis) river
Bottom: The Neviazhe (Nevėžis) river

יזכר

פארשטארבענע לאנדסלייט און מיטגלידער פון קיידאנער סאסייטי
תנצב"ה

פרידלאנד, יחזקאל	טריווויס, וואולף	באנק, לייב
פרידלאנד, מתתיהו	יאפע, אלטער	בירגער, חיים
פרידלאנד, חיים וואולף	יארע, שלמה	בירגער, לייב
פרידמאן חיים וועלוועל	כהן–ליבערמאן, יצחק	בירגער, שמואל
צעסלער, אפרים	כהן–ליבערמאן, בנימין	בלאך, מאקס
צעסלער, טביה	כהן, אריה לייב	בלומענטאל, לואי
צעסלער, משה	כארנאס, נתן	בעקער, משה
קאפעל, דוד	כארנאס, נחום	ברויז, חיים
קאפעל, פ.	לינדע, משה יצחק	ברענער, בערל
קארף, י.	לינדע, יעקב	גאלדבערג, אהרן
קולווינסקי, אהרן	לינדע, חיים	גאלדבערג, וו.
קיידאנסקי, יוסף	לינדע, יצחק	דאטנאווסקי, משה
קירפיצניקער, מ.	ליפציק, ראובן	דאטנאווסקי, ברוך
קראווויצקי	ליפשיץ, ברוך	דאט, חיים
קראווויצקי, תנחום	ליפשיץ, צבי ה"ד	דאנגעל, אלטער
קראמער, חיים יעקב	ליפשיץ, אליעזר	רינאבורסקי, חיים משה
קראמער, נחמיה	ליקער, מ.	הורוויץ, שלום
קראסט, חיים	ליקער, א.	הירשאוויץ, מ.
קראסט, הירשל	לעוויטאן, אבא	וואלפע, צמח
קראסט, זלמן	מאיערס, ל.	וואלפערט, משה לייב
ראזענבלאט, משה יצחק	מאנושעוויץ, אהרן	ווינער, י.
ראזענבלאט, יעקב	מארקונסקי, ישראל יוסף	ווינער, מרדכי
ראנדער, וואולף	מילנער, אליעזר	ווייצער, משה יהודה
ראנדער, אבא	מולער, משה יצחק	ווייצער, לייב
שאטער, שכנה	סוויניק, יעקב	ווייצער, איסר
שאיעוויץ, י.	סירקין, זעליג	ווערקסמאן, הירשע בער
שטיין, שמואל משה	סירקין, חיים לייזער	זוסמאן, לייזער
שטיין, זלמן	עפלשטיין, בן-ציון	טויב, יהודה
שמיט, יוסף	פאזאיצער, יצחק	טרויב, מיכאל
שלמה חאצע דער שמיד	פינקעל, משה ראובן	טרויב, הירשל
בערציק, יעקעס	פינבערג, ראובן	טרויב, וועלוול
לייבל אדעסער	פינבערג, וו.	טריווויס, בן-ציון

DECEASED LANDSLEIT AND MEMBERS OF KEIDANER SOCIETY
IN MEMORIAM

BANK Leib
BIRGER Chayim
BIRGER Leib
BIRGER Shmuel
BLOCH Max
BLUMENTHAL Louis
BECKER Moshe
BROIZ Chayim
BRENNER Berel
GOLDBERG Aharon
GOLDBERG V
DATNOVSKY Moshe
DATNOVSKY Boruch
DATT Chayim
DANGEL Alter
DINABURSKY Chayim Moshe
HORWITZ Sholem
HIRSHOWITZ M
VOLPE Tzemach
WOLPERT Moshe Leib
WEINER Y
WEINER Mordechai
WEITZER Moshe Yehuda
WEITZER Leib
WEITZER Isser
ZUSMAN Leizer
TOIB Yehudah
TROIB Michoel
TROIB Hirshel
TROIB Velvel
TREIVIS Ben Zion
TREIVIS Wolf

YAFFE Alter
YAREH Shlomo
COHEN – LIEBERMAN Yitzchak
COHEN – LIEBERMAN Binyomin
COHEN Aryeh Leib
CHARNAS Natan
CHARNAS Nochum
LINDE Moshe Yitzchak
LINDE Ya'akov
LINDE Chayim
LINDE Yitzchak
LIPCHIK Reuven
LIFSCHITZ Boruch
LIFSCHITZ Tzvi
LIFSCHITZ Eliezer
LIKKER M
LIKKER A
LEVITAN Abba
MAYERS L
MANUSCHEWITZ Aharon
MARKUNSKY Yisroel Yosef
MILNER Eliezer
MULLER Moshe Yitzchak
SUVEINIK Ya'akov
SIRKIN Zelig
SIRKIN Chayim Leizer
EPPELSHTEIN Ben Zion
POSITZER Yitzchak
FINKEL Moshe Reuven
FEINBERG Reuven

FRIEDLAND Yechezkiel
FRIEDLAND Matityahu
FRIEDLAND Chayim Wolf
FRIEDMAN Chayim Velveh
TZESLER Efraim
TZESLER Tevyeh
TZESLER Moshe
KOPPEL Dovid
KOPPEL P
KARP Y
KULVINSKY Aharon
KEIDANSKY Yosef
KIRPITZNIKER M
KRAVITSKY Tanchum
KRAMER Chayim Ya'akov
KRAMER Nechemyah
KROST Chayim
KROST Hirshel
KROST Zalman
ROZENBLATT Moshe Yitzchak
ROZENBLATT Ya'akov
RONDER Wolf
RONDER Abba
SHATTER Sachneh
SHAYEWITZ Y
SHTEIN Shmuel Yosef
SHTEIN Zalman
SHMIET Yosef
SHLOMO Chatzeh Der Shmied
BERTZIK Yekkes
LEIBEL Odesser

THE LATE MR SAMUEL STEIN   Pioneer and Philanthropist

The late Mr Samuel (Shmuel-Moshe) Stein, one of the foundation members of the Keidaner Society was a South African pioneer and highly respected member of the Johannesburg Jewish Community.

Mr Samuel Stein

Mr Stein and his wife Mrs Mary Stein have closely identified themselves with the life of the community ever since their arrival here from Keidan nearly 50 years ago. They made worthy contributions to all charitable and Jewish national institutions and organisations. They were well known as philanthropists and took particularly a keen interest in the work and activities of the Keidaner Society of which Mr Stein served for many years as chairman and treasurer. Mr Stein was a life member of this Society.

Mr Stein was born in 1877 in Amdur (near Grodno). His father was a prominent member of the Jewish community and was by trade a builder-contractor. His son Samuel received his Jewish education in the Cheder and Yeshiva in Grodno.

In 1894 Mr Samuel Stein settled in Keidan and in 1899 married Mary Kulvinsky the daughter of Hirsh Kulvinsky, a great Jewish Scholar of Keidan.

Mr Stein arrived in South Africa in 1903 and soon he became famous as a master builder. He made a valuable contribution to the progress of the building industry in the Golden City. During his lifetime he built eight Synagogues, the first Reform Temple in SA "Temple Israel", and apart from erecting thousands of modern and beautiful homes he was the building contractor of some of the City's most imposing sky-scrapers and blocks of flats, including London House, Pasteur Chambers, Polliack's Corner, Medical Centre, Ingram's Corner, also Gleneagles and Bretton Woods, the largest block of luxury flats in Johannesburg.

Mrs Mary Stein

Mr S. Stein also built some of the largest buildings in Durban including the Hotel Edward and Mayfair Hotel.

Mr Stein was a life member of the Beth Hamedrash Hagadol, a foundation member of the Muizenberg Talmud Torah, a committee member of the Witwatersrand Jewish Aged Home as well as a long standing member of the Great Synagogue, the Chevrah Kadisha, The Jewish Benevolent Society and various other organisations. An annexe of Herber House is named after Mr Stein in appreciation of his generosity and interest in Jewish education. This includes a bursary at the Seminary tenable for ten years.

Mr Stein donated an amount of £5,000 towards the building of Homes in Israel for immigrants from Keidan of which the Keidaner Society is the sponsor.

In February 1949, Mr and Mrs Stein celebrated their Golden Wedding anniversary and received numerous congratulations from many organisations and personalities. The Keidaner Society organised a special function on the occasion and inscribed Mr and Mrs Stein in the Golden Book of the Jewish National Fund.

Later in the year Mr Stein visited Israel and together with Mr S Keidan and Mr I Wolpe, members of the Committee of the Keidaner Society, negotiated with the directors of the Jewish National Fund concerning the allocation of land for the building scheme of houses for the Jewish immigrants from Keidan.

Mr Stein died on the 4th July, 1949. His death was an irreparable loss for the Community in general and for the Keidaner Society in particular.

Mr Max Stein, son of the late Mr S Stein is an active member of the committee and chairman of the Relief Fund of the Keidaner Society.

THE STEIN FAMILY IN THE US

Mr and Mrs David Stein (below left), the well-known communal workers and philanthropists who recently visited the Union and were guests of his late brother, Mr Samuel Stein of Johannesburg.

Mr David Stein, Mr Barnett Stein and their late mother

Mr and Mrs David Stein

Mr Barnett Stein

ZVI LIPSCHITZ, HY"D Ben-Moshe (Johannesburg)

The young Zvi Lipschitz, from Kfar Etzion, was a Keidaner landsman. He was born in 1919 in the town of Yasven (Josvainiai), near Keidan, and came to South Africa in 1934. He was a member of the local "Hapoel Hamizrachi" and in 1945 he left for Eretz Yisrael. He was killed on 4 Iyar, 5708 [May 13, 1948] during the heroic defense of Kfar Etzion. Zvi was a son of Baruch and Alte Lipschitz from Johannesburg. His father died in Johannesburg around the same time that his son fell in Eretz Yisrael.

When I remember Zvi Lipschitz, I recall someone I thought of both as my friend and as my rabbi; my friend who believed in the Zionist idea and the rebirth of a Jewish state, and my rabbi whose soul burned with enthusiastic fervour and devotion to his ideals.

He still looms before my eyes as in life. His finely chiselled, elegant head, the black locks of hair that were always a bit tousled and the deep, black, melancholy eyes that were always overcast with a thin mist.

I believe our first meeting took place right after he joined the Hapoel Hamizrachi party. He approached me for advice about his secular education. He had plans to go to university and thereby, as he expressed it, seek a synthesis between Judaism and secular knowledge. Not having the opportunity to carry out that plan he decided to undertake university studies on his own. I gave him the necessary books and he, with diligence and enthusiasm, threw himself into the work. I was impressed by his great ability, and I proposed to try to arrange for his admittance to university. But he came to me one day and said, "It is no use." His future was tied to Eretz Yisrael, and therefore it was his duty to learn a trade that would be useful in the building of the land. He decided on carpentry. Yet he did not abandon his dream of obtaining a wider education, and he continued to read and learn. In that time he was also participating actively in the Hapoel Hamizrachi movement, whose activist and missionary he became. I often heard his lectures to grownups and young people. How much passion, how much conviction and faith did he impart to them. Whether his listeners agreed with him or not, they were always carried away by his enthusiasm.

Speeches alone weren't enough for Zvi Lipschitz, however. For him his ideal was as real as life itself, and it gave him the thirst for life. He decided to leave for Eretz Yisrael. And although his movement was sorely in need of such an important and devoted activist, he received its blessing to follow through with his plan. He traveled to Eretz Yisrael and settled in

Zvi Lipschitz

Kfar Etzion – one of the hardest and most dangerous kibbutzim in the land, surrounded by innumerable hostile Arab villages. The kibbutz had already been destroyed once by the Arabs, but this did not stop Zvi from choosing such a dangerous outpost.

For a short time I took great pleasure in his frequent letters, which he would write to many of his friends, and later fate brought us together in Eretz Yisrael. I visited him a few times in Kfar Etzion. Each of those visits is engraved in my memory, because it revealed to me the other Zvi, not the dreamer and inspirer, but the builder and creator. I remember his heavy, confident pace as he walked his land, his devotion and pride in each tree growing in the hilly desert, in each building that appeared on the stony hill of Kfar Etzion. He was particularly concerned with construction, and the last time I saw him he was busy with building a shed, which would also serve as a strategic point in case of Arab attack. I remember well how he described how they had tested a heavy machine gun against the special blocks of concrete used during construction. He spoke about the defence of the kibbutz, and about matters which, in those times, under the terror of the British power, were to be kept strictly secret. That was our last intimate conversation, and fate decided that defending the kibbutz was also to be his last deed. He fell amid the burning ruins of the kibbutz together with more than 100 of his comrades, who gave their young, blossoming lives in the defence of the holy hills of Hebron. May God avenge his blood.

GREETINGS TO THE KEIDANER LANDSMANSCHAFT IN JOHANNNESBURG

FROM THE KEIDAN SOCIETY IN NEW YORK.

Esteemed friends and landsleit

As President of the Keidaner Society in New York, and also as a landsman, I have the honour to send you greetings for your fiftieth Jubilee, in my name and in the name of your friends and landsleit, members of the New York Society.

It is truly a great joy to be allowed to live to celebrate a fiftieth anniversary, especially that of an organisation which has endured so many turbulent times. It is indeed a great pleasure to see such an organisation, which managed to achieve so many great things in friendship, brotherhood and kindness, having been founded a half a century ago, by a small number of people who emigrated from a small shtetl in Lithuania, called Keidan.

The good deeds which you have accomplished during the fifty years of your existence, have reverberated throughout the Jewish, throughout the Jewish Press, by reports from the landsleit who have visited you. Also from your leaders, with whom we had the personal honour and pleasure to meet. But most particularly, from the mouths of the desperate brethren, who had the good fortune to escape the World Catastrophe.

We are not the only ones who are proud of you; the whole Jewish World can boast of an organisation such as yours. You have quite rightly chosen the name : "The Refuge for the Downtrodden of Keidan", which you have truly earned. May you be blessed.

Greetings to you from our Keidaner landsleit. Continue with your efforts as before. Your descendants will be proud of the gift which you bequeath them.

We would have dearly wished to have the pleasure of joining you and participating in your Simcha. Unfortunately, at this time, the "Keidaner Wooden Bridge" is not long enough to reach you. We too are occupied in making preparations for our own 50th Anniversary on 10 September 1950, to which we invite you.

Philip Grinblatt
President of the Keidaner Society
New York   10 April 1950

FROM THE HOLOCAUST SURVIVORS OF KEIDAN

Greetings from the Holocaust Survivors of Keidan to The Keidaner Society in Johannesburg on the Occasion of their 50th Jubilee Celebration.

I send you greetings and felicitations in the name of all the Keidaner landsleit, the Holocaust Survivors, in Germany, for the Jubilee of the Keidaner Society in Johannesburg.

Dear brothers of our destroyed town, may your hands be strengthened in the worthy work you do, to aid your desolate and homeless landsleit.

We have been made proud by your warm hearted response to date. We will also, surely, be made proud of you and your good deeds when we receive your magnanimous aid in the future.

May you be blessed in all your efforts for the good of the community and the individual.

Signed :
Dovid Volpe.

FROM THE KEIDANER IN SWITZERLAND

In the name of all the Keidaner in Switzerland, I would like to express my hearty good wishes to you for your 50th Jubilee .

Your expertise, in your outstanding, often difficult tasks, will assure your success in future endeavours, also in your achievements in the realm of brotherly assistance and sustaining the holy duty which has been made incumbent on you, and which you have been fulfilling for a half a century.

That is why we wish for a positive outcome, when every single Keidaner who has been uprooted will reach his goal.

May your landsmanschaft continue to serve as an example to other landsmanschaften, as it has done till now.

At this time, let us also not forget the Keidaner Jewry which has been annihilated and which was a predominant influence in the survival of the spirit of Torah and Judaic wisdom, in Lithuania.

We are therefore, also very proud, that you are participating in the rebuilding of Israel, where you want to perpetuate the name of Keidan.

Leizer Volpe

We also wish you much success and Mazal-Brocha in your future enterprises.

With best and heartiest greetings to all your landsleit, and best wishes for the future, in the name of all the Keidaner in Switzerland.

Leizer Volpe   Davos 1950

GREETINGS FROM THE "AFRIKANER YIDDISHE TZEITUNG" THE AFRICAN JEWISH NEWSPAPER

Esteemed friends,

It is with pleasure that we accept the invitation to participate in your Simcha, celebrating the 50th Anniversary of your landsmanschaft, in Johannesburg.

We especially wish to applaud the dedication and heartfelt sentiments which always reigned among the Keidaner landsleit, resulting in a truly fraternal association.

It would not be fair to shut our eyes and to ignore the direction in which Jewish societal and congregational life in South Africa has been tending in the past 20 years. Alas, the number of our "heimeshe" Lithuanian Jews is shrinking and lessening here, in this country. Even more so, we have lost and are losing many of them in the ever widening sea of assimilation, brought on by the innovations here.

The restricted immigration, prior to the previous World War rarely brought a Lithuanian landsman to the borders of South Africa, but the local landsleit received a much greater blow from the horrific Holocaust in Europe, in which the Pride of World Jewry was annihilated, Jewish Lithuania, together with its incomparable traditional and cultural treasures.

Jewish towns and shtetlach were wiped out in the Holocaust – centres of Jewish learning and wisdom, bastions of the Jewish spirit, like Telz, Slabodka, Shavell, Zager, Poneveszh, and others, among which also your beloved hometown, Keidan.

The Lithuanian landsmanschaften, which were established here, years ago, found themselves in a parlous situation under these new circumstances. The need to help the few surviving landsleit became huge and very urgent. The Jewish community was not very organised at the time, but this motivated local landsmanschaften to come to the aid of their ruined brethren in a much greater measure. We are aware that your brotherhood brought actual practical aid to them and made pragmatic plans to rehabilitate your unfortunate landsleit.

Our Jewish newspaper, which serves the interest of South African Jews in general, and Lithuanian landsleit in particular, is happy to participate in the celebration of 50 years of achievement with you. We hope that together with us you will always experience the connection to our ancient home and strive together for the progress of Jewish cultural life.

(signed) BORIS GERSHMAN.

GREETINGS FROM THE KEIDANER IN BEIT ZERA.
KIBBUTZ HASHOMER HATZA'IR
BEIT ZERA.

WORKERS FOR COMMUNAL SETTLEMENT (PTY) LTD IN K'FAR NATAN LASKY
4TH MAY 1960

The Keidaner landsleit in Kibbutz Beit Zera (Jordan Valley – Israel), as also Kibbutz Beit Zera, send hearty greetings to the Keidaner Society in Johannesburg on the occasion of their 50th Jubilee. May you continue to forge ahead in your deeds for the good of Keidaner landsleit and also for Eretz Yisrael.

"More power to your hands"!

KIBBUTZ BEIT ZERA
KEIDANER LANDSLEIT IN BEIT ZERA

The descendants of Keidan in Beit Zera (Jordan Valley – Israel), as also the settlers of the kibbutz itself, send most heartfelt greetings to the society of expatriates of Keidan in Johannesburg, on the 50th anniversary of its founding.

We wish you success and may you continue in your fruitful efforts for the good of the landsleit from Keidan and also the good of the Land of Israel.

Descendants of Keidan in Beit Zera
Kibbutz Beit Zera.

The Consul General of Israel

I have much pleasure in congratulating you on this happy occasion. May you go from strength to strength.

E D Goitein
Consul General of Israel

S A Jewish Board of Deputies

It gives me much pleasure to send a message to your Society on the occasion of its celebration of fifty years of activity.

The Board is fully acquainted with the fine work done by your Society for its members. Moreover, we are deeply sensible of the fact that the value of associations such as yours transcend the immediate services they render to their members, for they are a concrete expression of the loyalty of the Jew to his tradition and past, bound up with his life in the old country. Even though times have greatly changed, there still remains a field of activity for Landsleit Societies. We hope that yours will go from strength to strength.

F Zwarenstein
Chairman Welfare Committee

"The Zionist Record"

The town of Keidan is associated with the name of the Gaon of Vilna and has figured in modern Jewish history as the birthplace of the number of prominent personalities. As one of the Jewish communities in Lithuania it has had its share in the good name which Lithuanian Jewry has won for itself in Jewish Life.

Landsleit from Keidan have played a prominent part in the up-building of communal life in South Africa.

Our best wishes are extended to them all on the celebration of their 50th Anniversary, which indicates that members of this Society have been amongst the pioneers of South African Jewry. May the memory of the exterminated community of Keidan serve as a torch of light to all your members and as an encouragement for further efforts.

C Gershater
Editor

"S A Jewish Times"

It gives me particular pleasure to send a message of congratulation and good wishes for the future on this auspicious occasion of the Golden Jubilee of the Keidaner Helping Hand and Benevolent Society. The Keidaner Society is one of the oldest "Landsmanschaften" in South Africa, and occupies a place of special affection in my heart. My late father was the Rabbi of Krok, which was only a few miles from Keidan, and for as long as I can remember, the relations between the two communities were of the friendliest: they worked together in harmony, and in a spirit of brotherly collaboration. Another link I have with Keidan is the fact that it was from that district that the illustrious family of the Vilner Gaon came: as a great-great-grandchild of the Vilner Gaon, I have the same affection for Keidan as for my own birthplace.

Keidan always had an enviable reputation in Lithuania as one of the outstanding Jewish communities in the great Kibbutz, from which the majority of South African Jewry has come. I take this opportunity of congratulating the Keidaner Landsleit in South Africa for the noble manner in which they have kept up the traditions of their fathers, and I wish them every success in their endeavours to perpetuate the glorious name of Keidaner Jewry, which perished with the rest of Lithuanian Jewry in the Nazi Churban, al Kiddush Hashem.

Mr Leon Heldberg
Editor

MORE GREETINGS

Chairman's Greetings

Mr Max Stein

Fifty years ago a few immigrants from Keidan, finding themselves in Johannesburg, then a small city with whose inhabitants they had for the most part little in common and whose language and habits were naturally strange, banded together for mutual protection. In memory of the far distant town whence they came, they called this group "The Keidaner Society", and in the years that followed they were joined by other venturesome Keidaners and the Society grew bigger and stronger.

It is not necessary for me to make any other special reference to the history of the Society whose growth and development is a sufficient testimonial of its progress. The Society has a splendid record of accomplishments and its many good deeds are well known. It has been fortunate in having been served by capable and hardworking office bearers who never, even at great personal sacrifice, failed to render the utmost of their exertions, and I, quite new to my office, can only pledge myself to endeavour to emulate the high example set by many illustrious predecessors. I welcome this opportunity, on the occasion of the 50th anniversary of the Society's foundation, to greet my fellow members, to thank them for the honour paid to me in appointing me Chairman of the Relief Fund of our beloved fraternity, and to wish the Society continued success. May it always enjoy the same high esteem in which it has throughout its long existence been held by the community.

Max Stein

Message from the Chairman of the Ball Committee

Mr A Levin

It gives me great pleasure and I deem it a privilege to extend to all our friends gathered here tonight a warm welcome to our Golden Jubilee Ball.

The aims of the organisers of this ball are two-fold: Firstly, to celebrate the 50th Anniversary of the Keidan Society and, secondly to raise funds to enable us to continue with our relief and reconstruction in Israel for the benefit of our surviving brethren.

I wish to express my thanks to the Ball Committee and all members for their co-operation and assistance in making the Jubilee Ball a great success socially and financially.

I also take this opportunity to express our thanks to all the advertisers in our Souvenir Book for their patronage.

I greet you all and sincerely trust that you'll thoroughly enjoy yourselves.

A Levin

The South African Zionist Federation

The good work your Society has consistently performed over a period of fifty years is a fine achievement of which you can be justly proud.

If today your Society still serves a most useful function, notwithstanding that over the last decade the number of landsleit who have come to this country has been negligible, how important must have been your work fifty years ago when the Keidan Helping Hand and Benevolent Society was founded.

It was a great service you rendered then, to your landsleit who arrived in this country without money and with no knowledge of the language. You made them welcome, you helped to establish them and you made it possible for them to bring out their families. They, in turn, have played their part in building the fine community we have in this country.

But not only has your Society confined itself to work among your members, you have joined nobly in all phases of communal activity and development.

For these reasons it is with the greatest pleasure that on behalf of the S A Zionist Federation I give you our heartfelt congratulations on your Golden Jubilee. I wish you every success in all your activities.

Bernard Gering
Chairman

South African Ort-Oze

On the occasion of your Golden Jubilee the South African Ort-Oze sends you warmest greetings and best wishes.

In the communal life of South African Jewry the "Landsmanschaften" societies play a very important part, both in charitable and social endeavour: among them. Your Society in the last 50 years has been very prominent, and we of the Ort-Oze look forward to your continued efforts on behalf of the community.
Once again wishing you all the best.
Yours very truly

A Shaban
Chairman

PROMINENT KEIDANER SOCIETY MEMBERS SEND GREETINGS

Samuel Keidan

Barney Krost

H Schlapobersky

Chaim Geben

B Saloner Hon Life President

Michael Gladstone

Chaim Dangel

Berel Cohen

Zalman Kaplan

GREETINGS AND PHOTOS

Mr and Mrs Max Cohen

Mr and Mrs Z Bank

Mr and Mrs I Wolpe

Mrs Golde Lipchick and family

Mr and Mrs Max Cohen and family and Mr and Mrs Berl Cohen

Mr and Mrs J Goldberg and family

Mr R Rabinowitz

GREETINGS AND PHOTOS continued

Mr and Mrs E Berman

Mr and Mrs M Katz

Parents and Family of Mrs M Katz

Rocheh Bierman (Bereh Hendel's)

Ch Solomon

R Pokroy

Mr and Mrs B Bank

Mr and the late Mrs N Brenner and family

The late Mr and Mrs E Gordon and Family

Mr H Schlapobersky and his late father

A LETTER FROM THE KEIDANER LANDSLEIT IN ISRAEL   BEIT ZERA

Very esteemed and dear Keidaner Landsleit

We have received your letter, in which we read with great interest that you have accepted our suggestion of how to transfer the money to us to facilitate the building of a cultural centre in memory of the Martyrs of Keidan.

We send you herewith a plan for the institution. Together with this, is a specification page, showing how the institution will be sub-divided, for example: A reading room, a Hall "The Hall of the Martyrs", verandas etc.

Obviously we will consider your comments concerning the grounds and the layout of the building gratefully, and with much attention to detail. The large Hall (with the six windows), will also be used by us – the Keidaner Landsleit, in Israel - to assemble every year on the 5th of Elul, the yohrtzeit of the gruesome death of the Martyrs of Keidan, to commemorate their holy memory.

****

THE "KEIDAN MEMORIAL HOUSE" IN ISRAEL IN MEMORY OF THE MARTYRS OF KEIDAN

The "Keidan Memorial House" which will be erected on the banks of the Jordan in Beth- Zera, Israel, in memory of the Martyrs of Keidan. The "Memorial House" will consist of a Hall (which will be used for meetings, lectures, concerts and as a Reading Room) and a smaller Hall to be known as "Keidan Temple". The "Keidan Temple" will house documents, books and pictures dealing with Jewish life in Keidan and Its destruction.

The Foundation Stone of the "Keidan Memorial House" in memory of the late Mr. Samuel Stein will be laid in the near future by his son Mr Max Stein.

When the building is completed, we will invite all Keidaner, wherever they may be, to send us all notebooks, pictures and mementos pertaining to Keidan. We will look after them carefully, with great attention and devotion in the "Keidaner Temple" in Beit Zera.

Dear landsleit, we hope to remain in close contact with you and to continue to confer with you about the progress in the construction of the project. Our dearest wish, is that this institution should be a worthy monument in holy remembrance of the martyrs of Keidan.

You, on your part, should strive to make it possible for us to begin the building of this project, as soon as possible. The sooner, the better.

Heartiest greetings from the Keidaner Landsleit, and from all acquaintances and friends in Beit Zera.

In the name of the Keidaner Landsleit in Beit Zera

Pesach Chittin – Weitzer
Chairman

Reunion of a well-known Keidanian family on the occasion of the

Centre – Saruch and Grune Kagan (Kedainiai) their children and grandchildren.
First Row from Left – Aron David and Rachel Kagan, Morris and Bertha Udelson, Abraham A and Pesha Kagan.
Second Row – Dr Meyer and Clara Bernstein, Chas M and Rose Kane (New York).

Golden Wedding Anniversary of the Late Mr and Mrs Saruch and Grune Kagan

Third Row – Leon and Gertrude Kahn (Sacramento, Cal) Gutman and Masha Kagan, Boris and Bertha Cohen (Durban, South Africa). Samuel I and Sarah L Kagan, Max and Shime Cohen (Johannesburg, South Africa).

ADVERTISERS

- Acme Clothing Manufacturers Pty Ltd
- Dominion Wholesalers Limited
- Cutrite Clothing Manufacturers Pty Ltd
- Eagle Trading Pty Ltd
- Soll Clothing Manufacturers
- I Alter and Co Pty Ltd
- Crittall-Hope Metal Windows (SA) Ltd
- Cedar Brand Products
- Buirski & Binkin Pty Ltd - Drapers
- Sand & Co Ltd
- Progress Knitting Mills Pty Ltd
- Sydmac Metals
- Katzev & Perlstein - Decorators
- Precious Metals Development Pty Ltd
- Automobile Glass Works
- Datnow's Leather Works
- Carmel Hotel Warmbaths
- Celrose Limited - Knitwear
- Furman Glass Co Limited
- Ambassador Steam Pressers Pty Ltd
- Max Rainer & Co Ltd
- Jeppe Plumbing & Sheet Metal Mnfs Pty Ltd
- Cohen & Sons (Johannesburg) Ltd - Timber, Iron and Hardware
- Express Furniture Manufacturers
- A Miller Picture Framers
- Famous Czechoslovakian Factories for Sheet Glass
- United Dress Manufacturers
- Robert Nemen & Co Electrical Engineers
- Klo-Bri Products Pty Ltd
- Greenstein & Rosen Pty Ltd – Fancy and soft goods
- Mrs R Segal
- S A Wood-turning Mills – Occasional Furniture
- Sam Melman – Property and Insurance agent
- Moshal Gevisser & Partners Ltd
- Getz Bros South Africa Pty Ltd – Representatives
- Wire Industries Steel Products & Engineering Co Ltd
- H J Marks & Co – Wholesalers
- Johannesburg Spring & Mattress Works Pty Ltd
- Calu Industries Pty Limited – Paint and Putty
- Anglo-Alpha Cement Ltd
- S Malk Pty Ltd – Wholesalers and clothing manufacturers
- The Carpet Traders Corporation
- E I Rogoff Pty Ltd – Agents
- Standard Trading Co Pty Ltd – Soft Goods
- Lion Trading Co
- Rand Auctioneering Co
- Pretoria East Trading Company
- Pacific Oil Company Pty Ltd
- Progress Clothing Manufacturers
- South African Pine & Timber Co
- Mr & Mrs N Werksman and Family
- Shatterprufe Safety Glass Co Ltd Port Elizabeth
- Anglo African Shipping Co Limited
- S Stein & Sons (Tvl) Pty Ltd – Builders
- The Wearwell Shoe Company
- B Kopelowitz – Agents
- Fresh Meat Supply
- J C Cook & Cowan
- Plascon Quality Paints
- Shewitz Wholesalers Pty Ltd
- Hollard Investments
- Felt & Tweeds Ltd – Textile Manufacturers
- Steel & Barnett Ltd – Furniture Manufacturers
- G Cohen Pty Ltd – Wholesalers and Importers
- Unified Stone Crushers Pty Ltd
- National Venetian Blind Co
- Rockey Engineering & Wire Works Pty Ltd
- Central Agencies & Import Co Pty Ltd
- Primet Manufacturing Co
- Central Boot Factory 1943 Pty Ltd
- Universal Motors Limited
- South African Auctioneering
- Castle Hotel Warmbaths
- The Textile House Pty Ltd
- Saratoga Timbers Limited
- Berold and Busansky – Builders
- I Friedman Pty Ltd - Motor Body Builders and Spray Painters
- Clyde Trading Co Ltd - Builders' Hardware
- Plate Glass Bevelling & Silvering Co
- U Segell – Meats and Delicacies
- Polliacs - Musical and Electrical
- Primrose Brickworks 1936 Ltd
- Connock's SA Motor Co Ltd
- E Bilchik & Co Pty Ltd - Painters and decorators
- Koval Bros Pty Ltd – Refrigeration and Heating Engineers
- J H Isaacs & Co
- Economic Paint and Supply Store
- Rabro Florescent Manufacturing Co
- Max Cohen Painting Contractors
- African Gate and Fence Works Limited
- Frankfort Cold Storage – Eggs Butter Poultry
- Levy's Bakery
- President Wine and Brandy Co
- Levin & Company Wholesale Merchants
- S Lazarus & Co – Plumbing and Hardware
- Textile & General Holdings Limited
- Bailey's Delicatessen
- Epic Oil and Purene Vegetable Fat
- Pat Cornick & Co Pty Ltd - Spray Painters and French Polishers
- Fritz Rainer – Interior Beautifier
- Benoni, Brakpan and Springs Board of Executors and Trust Co Ltd
- Joseph Liddle Pty Ltd – Insurance
- South African Jewish Times
- Gollach & Gomperts Grain Merchants

I Goldsmith – Plumbing and Sheet Metal Worker
Express Glass Works Tvl Ltd
Wholesale Builders & Plumbers Suppliers
Marble, Lime and Associated industries Ltd
Israeli United Appeal
Max Gonski & Sons – Representatives
Levin's United Furnishing House Pty Ltd
Superior Furniture Manufacturers
S & L Motors Pty Ltd
Green Bros – Shippers, Export Merchants
Glazer Bros
Mr & Mrs Solly Yellin
S P Q R Stores – Grocers, Merchants and Importers
S Keidan & Co Pty Ltd – Builders
Tabatznik & Hochstadter – Painting Decorating
A Leo Meyer – Life Assurance
A B Silver & Co – Elect and Mechanical Engineers
Pheenie Sand & Co Pty Ltd –Cattle Feed
Johannesburg Motor Exchange
M Fihrer & Sons – Lime and Cement Manufacturers
Monica Hat Manufacturers
Veraat's Diamond Cutting Works Pty Ltd
Broudo's Saw Mill Pty Ltd
J C Farber Pty Ltd – Painting and Decorating
Frankel & Seehoff Ltd – Wholesale Merchants
B Jacobs Scrap & Machinery Merchant
Max Lewis (Maytex) Pty Ltd – Wholesalers and Clothing Manufacturers
F Roth – Glazing, Window Panes and Lead Lights
Darras Nurseries
S A Paper Processing Ltd
Brown Brothers Limited – Shippers
Art Fur Co Johannesburg
A Harris & Co Pty Ltd – Home and Office Furnishers
Penman & Jochelson Ltd – Electrical Engineers
Phoenix Plumbing Supplies Pty Ltd
Dominion Auctioneering Co
South African Meat Supply
Tiger Clothing Manufacturers Ltd
B & A Grolman & Co – Wholesale Merchants
Parry Leon & Hayhoe Ltd – Shipping Agents
Forsyth, Udwin Pty Ltd – Venetian Blinds
R E Pashley & Co Ltd - Statesman Shoes
Skinfit Pantie – a Kels Product
Harro Clothing Manufacturers Pty Ltd
Shopmaster Pty Ltd – Shopfitters
Benoni Crushers Pty Ltd – Screened Stones
Armourplate Safety Glass Pty Ltd
British Clothing Manufacturers
I Stein – Mining Material, Scrap and Metal Dealer
Clingman Bros & Co – Insurance Agents
Censor & Braudo Pty Ltd – Clothing Manufacturers and Merchants
The United Welding and Cutting Co Ltd
Gomex Pty Ltd – Wholesale and General Merchants
Premier Concrete Works

The Worsted House Pty Ltd – Woollen Merchant
Kaminer & Woolf – Builders
Bobrow Bros – Clothing
Dukes Bros Pty Ltd – Plastering & Grano Contractors
M Kalvin & Co – Builders' and Plumbers' Merchants
National Solder Co Pty Ltd
Bradlow Stores Ltd
Modern Upholsters
H Burde & Co – Plumbers', Builders' and Hardware Supplies
Industrial Crushers Pty Ltd
British and Overseas Insurance Company Limited
Victoria Shirt and Clothing Manufacturers
Rae's Bakery Pty Ltd
KaigorMnfg Co Pty Ltd - Kitchen Fittings
S Shavell &Co - Plumbers
Garet Cabinets Pty Ltd
Jaybee Brick Works
Berzak Bros Ltd - Textile Machinery
A J E Motors Pty ltd
M Stern - Building Industries
Sam Cohen - Windhoek
Krost Bros - Sheet Metal Products
J Goldberg - Building Contractors
Rand Pipes & Material Pty ltd
Phillip Karp
Springbok Steel Window and Engineering Co Pty Ltd
A Loewenthal Metals
Jacob & Salminis - Scrap Metal Merchants
E Rizzolio & Co Pty Ltd
Industrial Electrical Co Pty Ltd
Amalgamated Bricks Pty Ltd
Z Bank & Son - Builders and Contractors
Harry Gien Pty Ltd - Representatives
American Candy Works Pty Ltd
New Corner Service Station Pty Ltd
South African Metal Products Pty Ltd
Veneered Plywoods Pty Ltd
Perth Dry Cleaners & Launderers Pty Ltd
Modern Hairdressing Suppliers (Tvl) Pty Ltd
Standard Mineral Water Works
J H Ross & Co Pty Ltd
Cohen Goldman & Company - Shippers and Insurers
Pacific Press Pty Ltd
P G Timbers Ltd
G Cohan Pty Ltd Wholesalers and Importers
L & L - Woollen and Carpet Importers
Jules Murray Company Pty Ltd - Wholesalers
S A Crushers
S Seeff & Co - Estate & Insurance Agents
Edwin Wilson & Co Ltd - Representatives
Phoenix Brick Works
Wilfred J Kennedy Limited
Van der Stel Furniture Manufacturers Pty Ltd
Dandy Floor Polish

The original back cover of the book

Family Tree on classroom wall in Keidan - database from Andy Cassel

www.ingramcontent.com/pod-product-compliance
Lightning Source LLC
Chambersburg PA
CBHW051150290426
44108CB00019B/2676